GREATEST MOMENTS IN
OLE MISS
FOOTBALL HISTORY

EDITED BY FRANCIS J. FITZGERALD

CORPORATE SPONSORS

THE COCA-COLA BOTTLERS
OF MISSISSIPPI

HANCOCK BANK

SUPPORTING SPONSORS

C.C. Clark, Inc.	Johnny Baker	Mickey Holliman	Ronnie Parker
Starkville, Miss.	*Houston, Texas*	*Belden, Miss.*	*Dallas, Texas*

FL CRANE & SONS, INC.
Specialty Contractors

Campus Book Mart

McRAE'S
STYLE • QUALITY • SERVICE • INTEGRITY

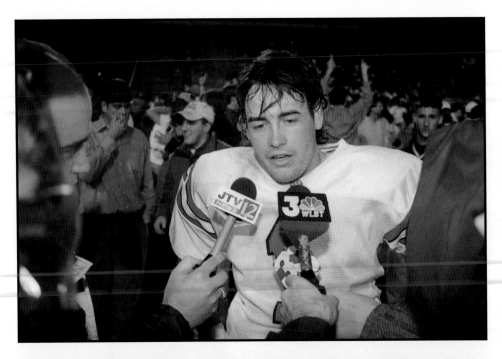

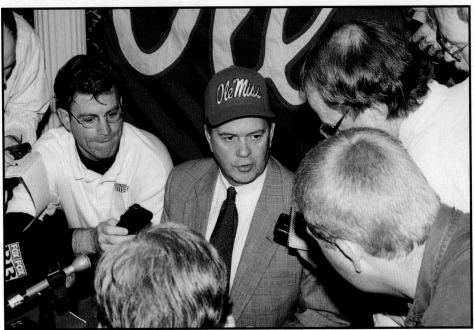

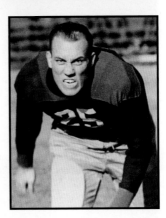

This book is dedicated to
John Howard Vaught
who built the foundation
of Ole Miss football

PHOTO CREDITS

AP/Wide World Photo: 158
Bruce Newman: 118, 135, 136, 137, 139, 140, 150, 152, 153, 159-right.
Louisiana State University Athletic Department: 56
Nokia Sugar Bowl: Front Cover, 51, 52-53, 53, 58-both, 59, 62, 64, 65-both, 67, 68, 69-both, 71, 95, 96, 97-both.
Southwestern Bell Cotton Bowl: 48-both, 49.
The Birmingham News: 73-all, 75, 76-both, 77, 80, 83, 84-both, 100-101.
University of Mississippi Archives: ii-left, 14, 16.

All other photographs courtesy of The University of Mississippi Athletic Department.

Acknowledgements: Langston Rogers and The University of Mississippi Sports Information Office, The Nokia Sugar Bowl, The Southwestern Bell Cotton Bowl, Texas Christian University, Louisiana State University, and the Paul W. Bryant Museum.

The feature story, *The Pooles of Poolesville USA*, is reprinted by permission of *Sport*.

ISBN# 0-928846-00-8 (softcover edition)
        0-928846-01-6 (hardcover edition)

Cover and Book Design: Lori Leath-Smith, Birmingham.
Photo Imaging: Lori Smith Design, Birmingham.
Typefaces: Big Blox, ITC Cheltenham Ultra Condensed, Minion MM.

CONTENTS

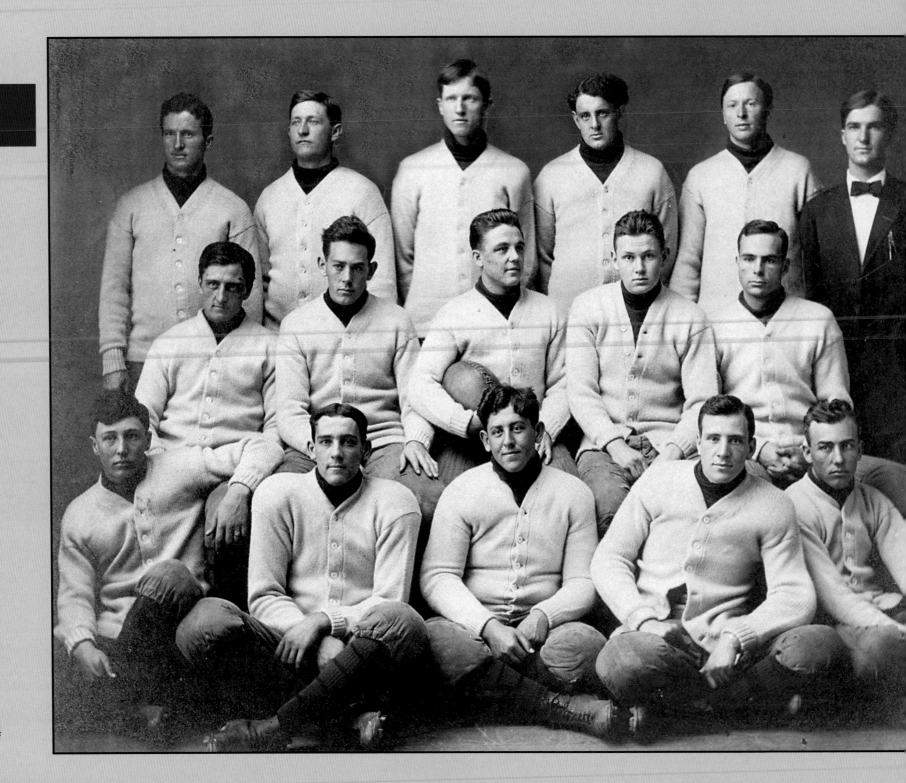

THE EARLY YEARS

"And then just before we went on the field to play, he laid it on the line. He got up steam pretty slowly, but by the time he got through to the ends and tackles and to the backs, he was really on charge."

OLE MISS TAILBACK PARKER HALL

15

The Rebels' 7-6 win over Mississippi State ended a 13-year losing drought.

Ole Miss 7 Mississippi State 6

November 25, 1926 | Starkville, Miss.

Ole Miss Halts State's 13-Year Win Streak

The Rebels overcame the Maroons of Mississippi State and buried a 13-year victory drought by defeating their traditional rivals, 7-6.

The winning drive began in the second quarter, when Ole Miss got the ball at midfield and in three passes reached the State 3-yard line. George Biles blasted through the Maroon line for the touchdown on the next play. Harvey Walker's extra-point kick gave Ole Miss a 7-0 lead.

State then countered by driving from their 30 to the Ole Miss goal line, but failed to convert the point-after kick which proved to be the margin of victory.

Several times the much-heavier Rebels marched deep into State territory, but the light Maroon troops stiffened.

State mounted a short-lived passing threat from their 15 which finished near midfield. Walker's interception of J.H. Meeks' pass intended for W.B. Ricks ended the threat.

Ole Miss	0	7	0	0 —	7
Mississippi State	0	6	0	0 —	6

The contest only had two penalties, both against Ole Miss. One for holding and one for roughing.

State barely led in first downs, 11 to 10. The Rebels controlled the air game with 7 passes for 109 yards while the Maroons had 4 passes for 64 yards. Ole Miss also intercepted three Maroon aerials.

A crowd of 10,000, which was almost evenly divided, turned out to watch this grudge match. The field was still slippery after the deluge of rain from the night before. Five train loads of Ole Miss fans had traveled from Oxford to cheer on their team.

At the end of the game, State fans sang their alma mater as the Maroon players walked off the field with heads bowed. Ole Miss fans tried to tear down one of the State goalposts but were not successful.

Ole Miss 14   Mississippi State 6

Nov. 30, 1935 | Oxford, Miss.

Hapes Paves Way Against Maroons In Thriller

Mississippi State's finest ball club of all-time was stopped by a feisty Ole Miss squad which continued its 10-year domination over the Maroon. A crowd of nearly 14,000 watched as a stronger Rebel squad rip 57 yards for a first-quarter touchdown, hold onto their lead after the Maroon scored in the fourth quarter, then captured victory with Ray Hapes' 90-yard touchdown run.

Big Clarence Hapes scored the Rebels' first touchdown after dazzling runs by Ray Hapes and Rab Rogers. The brilliant running of State's Ike Pickle and the pinpoint passing of Pee Wee Armstrong evened the score for the Maroon five minutes into the final quarter.

Then came the moment of drama. Bull Day, who had replaced Pickle, booted the Maroon's extra-point kick. It went high into the air, but veered left. In a fraction of a moment that seemed to last forever, the ball finally hit the left goalpost, and bounced back onto the field.

It was a staggering setback for State.

Mississippi State	0	0	0	6 —	6
Ole Miss	7	0	0	7 —	14

The stunned Maroon team was dealt another blow on the next play when Ray Hapes, who had been heavily covered on punts and kickoffs all afternoon, gathered the ball in at the Rebel 10 and raced upfield toward the State goal line. At the 30, he ran into a pack of Ole Miss blockers and State tacklers, but managed to escape untouched.

With only one opponent still in his way at midfield, Hapes slipped past him on a daring fake. Two State players tried to catch him at the Ole Miss 40, but Hapes managed to find an extra gear and legged it the Maroon end zone untouched. Bill Richardson booted the extra-point kick which gave the Rebels a 14-6 lead but State wasn't ready to quit.

They came fighting back. Armstrong fielded Dave Bernard's kickoff at the State 5 and sprinted straight upfield. And if he had been as fast as

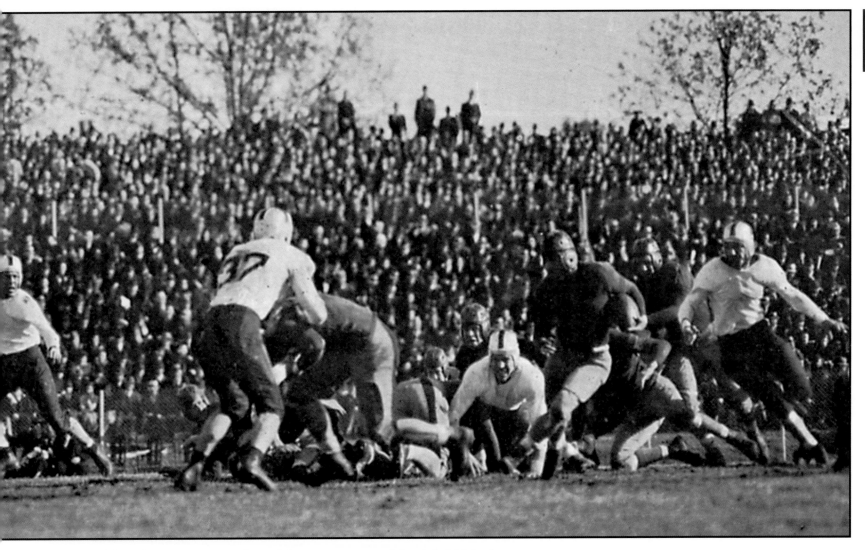

Ray Hapes' fourth-quarter 90-yard touchdown run ensured the Rebs' 14-0 win.

Pickle, he would have reached gloryland. But he wasn't. Richardson and Rogers brought him down at the Rebel 40 — and ended the Maroon's hopes.

State, under new coach Ralph Sasse, had already beaten Alabama and powerhouse Army at Yankee Stadium this season, but couldn't get past Ole Miss and take possession of the Golden Egg Trophy, which the Rebels have owned for ten seasons since the trophy was first presented in 1926.

Ole Miss 20   Louisiana State 7

Sept. 24, 1938 | Baton Rouge, La.

Ole Miss & Parker Hall Shock Vaunted Tigers

O le Miss bloodied the mighty LSU Tigers with a 20-7 whipping in their own backyard.

It was a fierce Rebel defense that fought back the Bengal's offensive firepower that battered the Ole Miss line and swept the ends which proved to be the difference in victory this afternoon.

It was Ole Miss' first win over LSU in eleven years and the eighth victory since 1894. It was also the Rebels' first Southeastern Conference win since defeating Mississippi State in 1935.

LSU failed to score in a first-quarter drive and never seemed to be able to keep up with the scrappy Rebels. The Tigers drove to the Ole Miss 15 but was halted by the Rebels' forward wall. Cotton Milner's field goal missed the mark.

On the Tigers' next drive, Earl Graham fumbled the ball after being hit.

Seizing the opportunity, Parker Hall drove the ball to midfield. He

Ole Miss	7	0	13	0 —	20
Louisiana State	0	0	0	7 —	7

then heaved a long pass to Ham Murphy at the LSU 10, who wasted no time in finding the Tigers' end zone. Kimble Bradley's point-after kick gave Ole Miss a 7-0 lead.

Hall scampered for long yardage in the third quarter to set up a touchdown and Willard Bisbing added another afterward. LSU eventually got a touchdown in the fourth quarter but it was too late.

The coaching prowess of Harry Mehre was perhaps the key in this new brand of Rebels. His ability to turn a once defeatist Ole Miss attitude into a roaring beast brings to mind the legendary skills of William Sherman, the Civil War general whose Yankee juggernaut marched through Georgia and later became president of Louisiana State when it was often called the Ol' War Skule.

Parker Hall, an All-American tailback, passed for 1 TD and set up another against LSU.

After Murphy's opening touchdown, LSU made drives to midfield and to the Ole Miss 30 but the Rebel defense stood tall.

In the third quarter, Hall fielded a LSU punt at the Ole Miss 48, ran to the left sideline but there was no running room there, then circled deep in his territory and headed for paydirt behind jolting blocking. He was tackled at the LSU one-foot-line.

On the next play, Bill Schneller, the Rebels' quarterback, carried the ball over for a touchdown. John Whittington added the extra-point kick to give Ole Miss a 14-0 lead.

LSU's John Stell then rumbled like a mad rhino, leading the Tigers to the Ole Miss 40. After being hit, the ball squirted from Stell's hands and Bisbing caught it in mid-air. He galloped untouched to the LSU goal line for the Rebels' third touchdown. Whittington's point-after kick failed. Still, Ole Miss led, 20-0.

Barrett Booth later intercepted an Ole Miss pass at the Tigers' 32. Finally, LSU began to growl. Young Bussey passed to Ogden Bauer at the LSU 43, who then sprinted to the Ole Miss 25. Robert Fife carried to the Rebels' 15. Moments later, Bussey dived over from the Ole Miss 1. Booth added the extra-point kick to reduce the Rebels' lead to 20-7.

Harry Mehre arrived from Georgia and quickly built the Rebels into a winner with a 9-2 record in 1938.

PARKER HALL: A Man in the Right Place

The year was 1938 in Tiger Stadium. It was not packed at all. And why should it have been?

In the past season, Ole Miss had won four games, lost five, tied one and lost a coach, the memorable Ed Walker.

In 1937, LSU, with Bernie Moore at the reigns, won nine games and lost one (to the Vandy Commodores, 7-6). Among the Tigers' victories was a 13-0 win over Ole Miss.

LSU was the favorite to go through the season undefeated and win the Southeastern Conference title. Ole Miss was the first stepping stone.

The stone was slippery. The guy who greased it was Parker Hall, a big tailback from Tunica, Miss., on an Ole Miss team that was rebuilding.

The score in 1938 was Ole Miss 20, LSU 7. Harry Mehre was the new coach in charge of the Rebels.

"We went down there all down and out," Hall explained when recalling that memorable trip to Baton Rouge. "We hadn't won a conference game the year before and we weren't confident of winning many that year.

"The team stayed in Hammond and we drove over to Baton Rouge on a bus. Coach Mehre was pretty nervous, smoked cigarettes from one end of the tip to the other. He explained to us that he had to quit smoking cigars because he used up eight or nine a game. There wasn't much doubt he was kind of tense.

"And then just before we went on the field to play, he really laid it on the line. He got up steam pretty slowly but by the time he got through to the ends and tackles and on down to the backs, he was really on a charge."

"That's the highest I've ever been and I guess it went for the whole team.

"Mehre planned to hit 'em a lick right at the start and I cracked up and threw a long pass to Ham Murphy and we were up, 7-0.

"Then I ran a punt back and got stopped on the LSU 1-yard line. Bill Schneller, our quarterback, took it over for the touchdown. And then Willard Bisbing (a halfback) intercepted a pass and we were up, 20-0. We knew they couldn't catch us.

"It was a good team, that LSU squad, with Young Bussey playing tailback, Ken Kavanaugh at end and Ben Friend at tackle. But Mehre said in the beginning we should win it and his talk put confidence in us, made us think we were better than we were.

"You can say we were pretty happy going back on the bus and naturally Mehre was happier than anybody."

The LSU game was a big one for Hall. The tailback from Tunica proved to be a passing and running whiz. He would be named all-America at the end of the 1938 season after the Rebels defeated Tennessee in Memphis.

The Rebs took a 9-1 record that day into Crump Stadium, having lost only to Vanderbilt. The Rebs had already beaten Arkansas, 20-14, and Mississippi State, 19-6.

Hall was later drafted to play for Cleveland in the pro league. There, he posted some team passing records and distinguished himself as an all-around performer.

THE VAUGHT ERA

"If I knew anyone could lead Ole Miss out of the wilderness, John Vaught was the one to do it."

OLE MISS ATHLETIC DIRECTOR TAD SMITH

Ole Miss 20   Louisiana State 18

November 1, 1947 | Baton Rouge, La.

Conerly's 3 Touchdowns Lead Rebs Over LSU

Charlie Conerly, the magnificent Ole Miss flamethrower, put on the finest passing exhibition in Louisiana since Davey O'Brien passed TCU to a Sugar Bowl win over Louisiana State in the 1939 Sugar Bowl.

With 46,000 on hand this evening in Tiger Stadium, no one left until the final buzzer. They didn't even carry out the ones with heart failure — they just stood on them in order to get a better view.

And Conerly didn't disappoint anyone. He personally crossed the LSU goal line three times to lead the Rebels to a 20-18 triumph.

But the Tigers were in this contest until the red and black hands on the end zone scoreboard clock both hit 12 at the end of this thrilling contest. LSU's final scoring threat was mounted with a minute 45 seconds left in the fourth quarter when they drove from their 47 to the Ole Miss 28. Conerly's openfield tackle of the Tigers' Jeff Adams ended LSU's hopes.

The Tigers were the winners in the stats totals. LSU had 22 first downs to Ole Miss' 9, outrushed the Rebs, 329 to 201, and outpassed

Ole Miss	0	13	0	7 —	20
Louisiana State	6	0	0	12 —	18

them, 130 to 121.

But the Tigers didn't have Conerly.

The Reb pitcher connected on 12 of 19 passes for 121 yards and carried the ball for 66 yards — 26 of these set up the Rebels' final touchdown which made the difference.

Conerly ran two more yards over left guard for six more points. He added six more points on a 2-yard blast. Little Bobby Oswalt's steady toe booted both of the Rebels' extra-point kicks.

The Rebels fielded the opening kickoff at its 33, but got off to a slow start. Conerly passed to Red Jenkins which ended up in a two-yard loss. Conerly was sacked for a 12-yards loss on the next play. On third down, he then punted to the LSU 46.

At that point, LSU was off to the races. Y.A. Tittle threw for 9 yards to

Jim Lyle and Rip Collins blasted off-tackle for four yards.

The Tigers got a bonus when Ole Miss was ticketed with a 15-yard roughing penalty which moved the ball up to the Reb 24. Tittle connected with Carroll Griffith on a 10-yard pass and then Griffith smashed over the middle for seven yards to reach the Ole Miss 1. Collins punched it over on the next play but Holly Heard's point-after kick failed.

The 1947 Rebels won their first Southeastern Conference title with a 9-2 record.

Conerly soon made his presence known. He flung an 18-yard aerial to Barney Poole, then lost 11 yards while trying to pass. Two plays later, Conerly quick-kicked 56 yards to the Tiger 33.

Tittle, who was trapped deep in his backfield, then threw to Dan Sandifer for 34 yards to the Ole Miss 33. Conerly, who was the only player between Sandifer and the Ole Miss goal made the saving tackle. Jenkins' interception of a Tiger pass ended the drive.

Early in the second quarter, Ole Miss marched from the Rebel 41 and scored in seven plays. Conerly crossed the goal line on a 2-yard dive. Franklin's point-after kick gave Ole Miss a 7-6 lead.

LSU took the kickoff at the Tiger 18. On the second play, Tittle fumbled and lost the ball. Bobby Wilson made the recovery and carried it to the LSU 11.

Conerly then threw for five yards and raced around left end for two yards. He covered the remaining distance to the goal line with a pair of Tigers clinging onto him. Oswalt's point-after kick failed.

The action didn't heat up again until early in the fourth quarter when

LSU got the ball at its 48 and marched to the Reb goal line in 10 plays. Collins scored on a 6-yard toss around right end. Although Heard missed the point-after kick, Ole Miss held onto a skinny 13-12 lead.

Conerly went to work. Beginning at the Ole Miss 27, Will Glover added 12 yards, then Conerly passed to Barney Poole at the 50, who ripped to the LSU 35. Conerly next passed to Jerry Tiblier for 15 yards. After a 6-yard loss by Dixie Howell, Conerly faked a pass, then raced to the LSU goal line. He went across dragging a Tiger player. Oswalt's extra-point kick gave Ole Miss a 20-12 lead.

But there was still life in the Tigers. LSU's Ed Claunch returned Poole's kickoff to the Ole Miss 47. Collins broke through left tackle for 14 yards. Tittle then faked and swept around right end for 19 yards. On the next play, he lateraled to Ray Coates, who rolled left and passed to Joe Leach in the end zone. Heard missed the point-after kick for the third time.

The Tigers tried to mount one more scoring drive but Ole Miss managed to hold onto a 20-18 lead.

Ole Miss 43   Tennessee 13

November 8, 1947 | Memphis, Tenn.

THE
VAUGHT
ERA

Too Much Conerly & Poole: Rebs Shatter Vol Myth

The legend of Charley Conerly grew larger this afternoon as he ended Tennessee's 45-year winning streak over the Rebels by throwing for four touchdowns and running for two more, allowing Ole Miss to stomp the Vols, 43-13, in front of a crowd of 28,000 at Crump Stadium.

After the game, Tennessee coach Robert Neyland noted, "Conerly is the greatest back I've ever seen."

It was Neyland's worst loss in his 21-year coaching career and the Rebels' first in this series.

Conerly dove over from the Vol 2 for the Rebs' first touchdown three minutes and 15 seconds after the game began. Bobby Oswalt added the point-after kick to give Ole Miss a 7-0 lead. Afterward, there was no stopping these Rebs.

The Vols responded at the start of the second quarter on a J.B. Proctor pass to Jim Powell for a touchdown. They were the winning combination in the Vols' victory last year. The extra-point attempt failed.

Ole Miss	7	15	14	7 —	43
Tennessee	0	6	0	7 —	13

Barney Poole's punt block for a safety boosted the Rebs' lead to 9-7. He later hurried a second punt.

Conerly got into high gear again. His passing quickly brought the Rebs up to the Vols' 5. He then sprinted around end for a touchdown.

The remaining touchdowns only added to Tennessee's misery.

The Rebs' third touchdown came on 34-yard pass to Earl Howell. Howell caught touchdown No. 4 and big Poole hauled in a difficult pass for No. 5.

Poole's daring reception was a catch for the ages. It began with a Conerly pass to Farley Solomon near the Vol goal line, but Tennessee's Bernie Milner knocked the ball toward the ground. Poole, however, made a dive toward the ball and pulled it in before it reached the ground and scrambled across the Vol goal line for the score.

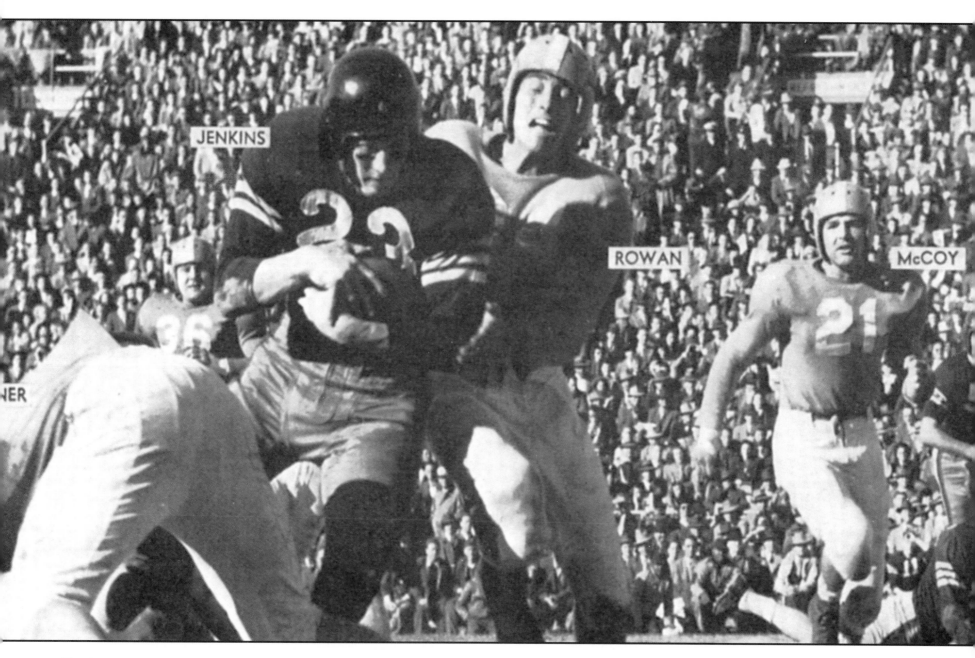

Fullback Red Jenkins (23) powers through the Tennessee line for 10 yards.

Barney Poole piles up Vol halfback Hal Littleford in the Rebs' 43-13 win at Crump Stadium in Memphis.

Billy Bowen caught Conerly's fourth touchdown pass which was his sixth touchdown overall — and final — for the afternoon.

The Vols got on the scoreboard once more in the final quarter when Ralph Huneycutt intercepted a Billy Mustin pass and ran 41 yards to the Reb end zone.

But it was too little, too late.

CONERLY & POOLE:
Reb Duo Struck With Thunder

For 45 years the mighty Vols had kept the Rebs in their place — with their heels firmly digging into the backs of the Ole Miss players.

But the Rebs finally overcame their past and with the deadly passing duo of Charlie Conerly and Barney Poole thrashed the Vols, 43-13, this afternoon. It was a beautiful sight.

Ole Miss and Tennessee first began playing in 1902. They had played 17 times before today, with the Vols winning 16 times and tying only once — in a 0-0 draw in 1936.

Conerly and Poole began to improve that count this afternoon. Conerly passed for 239 yards on 19 completions and four touchdowns and ran for a pair of touchdowns that put the Vols on the ropes.

He was an excellent chess master in football cleats.

And if Conerly isn't all-American, then neither is Douglas MacArthur.

Another who tied added an all-American notch in his belt today was Barney Poole, the big end, who blocked two Vol punts and made a leaping catch just as the ball was about to land on the end zone grass.

A pair of all-Americans: Charlie Conerly (42) and Barney Poole.

31

Ole Miss 13   Texas Christian 9

THE VAUGHT ERA

Ole Miss Bounces Back To Dehorn TCU Frogs

Charlie Conerly, playing in his last college game, rallied the Rebels to a fourth-quarter 13-9 victory over the TCU Horned Frogs this afternoon at Crump Stadium in the inaugural Delta Bowl.

Following the game, Conerly was awarded the country's "Best Player of the Year" by the Helms Foundation and *Sports Digest* magazine at a dinner at The Peabody Hotel.

TCU, which had not lived up to preseason expectations, battered the Rebels for a touchdown and a safety in the second quarter. By halftime, it must have seemed to the half-frozen crowd of 28,120 that the Rebs' comeback chances were slipping.

But Conerly & Co. didn't know how to give up.

In a five-minute period, Conerly tossed a pair of touchdowns — to Joe Johnson and Earl Howell — then personally halted the Frogs' last advance.

These two touchdowns and an extra-point kick by Bobby Oswalt overcame TCU cornerback Lindy Berry's interception for a touchdown

Ole Miss	0	0	0	13 —	13
Texas Christian	0	9	0	0 —	9

and a safety scored by Weldon Edwards when he blocked an Ole Miss punt.

TCU used a seven-man line to stop — or to slow down — Conerly, who was the No. 1 passer in the country in 1947.

In the third quarter, the Rebs' fortunes quickly changed. Ole Miss drove to the Frogs' 39, but after losing the ball on downs, TCU's Carl Knox let loose a 73-yard booming punt that pinned up the Rebs.

Eventually Conerly & Co. got loose and traveled to the TCU goal line in nine plays. Johnson snatched a pass from Berry's "intercepting" arms and fell over into the end zone which cut the Frogs' lead to 9-6.

Bobby Wilson, whose earlier pass was intercepted by Berry and returned for a Frog touchdown, got a chance at redemption when he stole a Pete Stout pass at the Ole Miss 36.

THE VAUGHT ERA

Barney Poole (89) leads the blocking while Dixie Howell (31) sweeps downfield for the Rebs' game-winning touchdown against TCU.

Wasting no time, Conerly found Johnson open on a route up the middle of the field and pitched a perfect 10-yard pass to him. He made it to the TCU 13 before Charlie Jackson caught up with him — a 51-yard gain.

The stunned Frogs weren't able to stop Howell when he romped over for the Rebs' game-winning touchdown. Oswalt's extra-point kick made it 13-9.

33

The Pooles of Pooletown, U.S.A.

By Bob Dunne

Sport, December 1948

The country's chief football factory isn't Notre Dame or Michigan or the University of Whathaveyou. It's a dusty little town in Southern Mississippi where the city limits sign say: "Gloster, pop. 1,100."

It might just as well read: "Pooletown, U.S.A."

For that's where the Poole boys live, and if there is a bigger and better footballing family in America, nobody's heard about it yet.

The tiny town is not on many maps. It's a bit more than 30 miles off the main highway that goes to the Gulf Coast. The people there make their living from cotton and lumber. But wander along Gloster's main (and only) business street and you'll wonder just what the most important products really are — cotton and lumber or athletes named Poole.

There's actually more comment on what Barney and the others are doing than there is about the price of cotton. And in Mississippi, brother, that's something!

There are four branches of the Poole family. While no one household has quite produced a full-fledged grid squad, put them together and the clan tree is draped from top to roots with husky lads who have won more honors in sports than the Aga Khan has jewels and racehorses.

Here's the lineup:

Barney Poole — all-American end with those great Army teams of 1944 to '46; the man who last year set an all-time record for pass snagging as the target for Chunkin' Charlie Conerly at the University of Mississippi; now playing his seventh season of collegiate ball.

Jim (Buster) Poole — All-Pro with the New York Giants, now an end coach with Ole Miss.

Ray Poole — another end currently performing at Buster's old post with the Giants; an ex-Ole Miss star.

They're brothers.

Then there are the cousins Oliver, a tackle with the Baltimore Colts; Jackie, Phillip and Leslie, linemen presently playing with Barney on the Ole Miss team; and Flemin, the former Mississippi mainstay and high school coach.

That so many members of this clan should become so successful in sports isn't as strange as it may seem. In the case of the Pooles, it's just "doing what comes naturally." Those are

THE VAUGHT ERA

Ray Poole (61), Oliver Poole (44), Phillip Poole (25), and Jackie Poole (24). Jackie and Phillip are brothers; Ray and Oliver are cousins.

Buster's words and the others agree.

Each and every one is a huge, towering bulk of brawn. And take a look at their parents.

There are six brothers, all hardy men of the soil, six-foot, 200-pounders. The folks around Gloster — like Mayor George Smith, a baseball enthusiast — remember the days when the whole town used to turn out to watch contests put on by the Pooles. They pitched horseshoes, played baseball and basketball, held foot races. They even made a sort of sport out of farming by setting up prizes for the Poole whose crops were bigger and better than his brothers' crops.

Their taste along some delicate lines ran in the same pattern, too. The father of Buster, Barney and Ray — Willie A. Poole — and his brothers, Hillery and Don, married a pair of sisters. Their brides were the Berryhill sisters of Gloster — tall, large, women who weren't afraid of a hard day's work in the fields.

But while the present generation inherited certain competitive aptitudes and physical assets, they didn't just grow up, go off to college, and become sports stars. It wasn't that easy. In fact, it was particularly difficult for Buster, Barney and Ray, whose achievements slightly overshadow the others'.

Their father, Willie Poole, died unexpectedly of a ruptured appendix at the age of 44. That left the widow, Emily, with a 180-acre farm, a partnership in a small saw mill, three sons and four daughters.

So nine-year-old Buster became the "man of the plantation." By the time he was 10, he had "turned in the crop, plowing all of the land by himself." Ray was a toddling three years old and Barney a babe in arms. They, too, went to work as soon as they became large enough to handle a hoe.

About the hardships and struggles of those years immediately after her husband's death, Mrs. Poole says: "The family simply took it in stride." A mighty sturdy stride it must have been.

The situation had improved when Buster had reached high school age. The farm land had been rented out and Mrs. Poole was hoping the children could get a complete education. But it was hard to see how. The nearby rural school offered only three years of prep study. It seemed that would be as far as the Pooles could go.

Then sports stepped in and lent a helping hand.

Busy though they were, the boys were athletes from childhood. There were always enough of them to choose up sides and play ball when the day's work was done.

It was a Poole pitching, a Poole catching and a Poole batting. Pooles all over the place.

One afternoon, a high school coach from Natchez, Miss., watched his basketball team lose to a little rural quintet led by a brawny forward named Buster Poole. Impressed, the coach talked to Buster after the game and asked what other sports he played.

"Baseball and ah'm pretty fair at horseshoes," was Buster's honest answer.

The area simply didn't have the facilities for football. As far as most folks were concerned, a pigskin was — well, it was a pig's hide, pigs is pigs, and that was that.

The coach made a bargain with Buster: "Come to Natchez with me and play with our teams. I'll find you a place to stay and you can get in that fourth year of school. The place to stay turned out to be practically a suite in one of the famous antebellum homes along the Mississippi River in Natchez.

Buster didn't like it. "Too rich for my country blood. I couldn't relax. Packed up and went home where I could walk around in my bare feet if I felt like it."

The coach chased after him. "Okay," he said. "I've got another place lined up. Made special arrangements with the sheriff." Buster's new home was a private cell in the Adams County jail. He liked it fine. "Got three good meals a day and could do almost as I pleased," he says.

Buster Poole, the Rebs' end coach, and his prize pupil (and brother), Barney Poole (89).

But when it came time for the county to make its regular check on expenses, the auditor found the jail had been dishing out more meals than it had prisoners. Buster had to leave but the ingenious coach finally found a permanent residence for his protege — a room over an old drug store.

IT WAS IN NATCHEZ that the eldest of the Pooles discovered football — or you might put it the other way around. Anyway, he was a natural end — the kind who doesn't get suckered in and who can leap over blockers and bring down the ball-toter.

Buster's rugged performance in his first year as a gridder at Natchez led him to the University of Mississippi on an athletic scholarship. When he graduated in 1937, he was awarded the university's Norris trophy as the school's outstanding athlete-scholar. Thus Buster started the saga of the Pooles at Ole Miss. He more or less opened the door for his brothers and cousins to step through. They all followed him to Ole Miss on athletic scholarships and the name Poole became a byword on the Rebel campus at Oxford.

Meanwhile, the word "sport" became magic to Mrs. Emily Poole. At 63, and still living on the same place, she looks back and says, "I'm mighty appreciative. Sports have given my sons, and the sons of my relatives, college educations. Don't see how they could've got them otherwise."

Like all mothers, she worries about the boys getting hurt. Not so much about Buster and Ray as about Barney. "You know," she says, "that Barney of mine just has a knack for getting broken noses and the like."

Even in those family games when they were kids, it was always Barney who wound up looking as though he had been run through a cotton gin. There's one incident the whole family recalls. Buster was with the Giants and 15-year-old Barney was playing a sandlot game back home. Barney blocked four punts in that one afternoon. When Buster got a letter about it, he says he bragged for a week about "that kid brother of mine back in Mississippi." Then he received another letter. Barney was laid up with appendicitis — a case of catching too many punts in the stomach.

Buster told his teammates about this and Ken (Kayo) Lunday, a guard on the Giants, decided; "That boy hasn't got appendicitis. He's got a football on his ribs."

Barney's known to the family as "The Kid" and that's not merely because he's the youngest. In Buster's words; "He's an overgrown boy, easy-going, laughing all the time. He'll finish a three-hour workout and later you'll find him playing tag with the other kids in the neighborhood."

"The Kid" is a 220-pounder, six-foot-three (like Buster and Ray) and is 24. It appears that his accomplishments are going to make him the best player the Pooles ever produced.

One of the high spots of his career was as a slashing wingman with Blanchard & Davis Inc. at West Point for three years. But he also ran into rough luck at Army, becoming a scholastic casualty in his senior year.

Going back to Mississippi, where he started in 1941, Barney says he "went all out for flunking out of the Point." It seems he has. Last year, he and Chunkin' Charlie formed the most prolific pass-completion team in the history of college ball. Barney grabbed 52 of Charley's aerials and turned them into 511 yards gained and eight touchdowns. He made first team on 12 all-American teams and Ole Miss won the Southeastern Conference championship for the first time.

This Spring, Barney received his bachelor's degree in Physical Education and is now working for his master's. He married a childhood sweetheart, Martha Carney — black-haired, "cute" and five-foot-five. The wedding was held in Gloster last July and, needless to say, the church was packed with Pooles.

MARTHA AND BARNEY set up housekeeping in Gloster but have moved to Oxford for his final year of school. One of the neighbors is Buster, with his wife, Anna Rose, and their three-year-old daughter, Joanna.

Good neighbors, Buster and Barney agree that "the family gets along nicely." The Pooles on the Mississippi squad look up to Buster as the senior member of the clan and, as end coach, the boss on the gridiron as he used to be long ago in the fields.

Naturally, Coach Poole can't afford to give a prejudiced portion of his instructions to his relatives. But they all get a chance to review plays and tactics as neighbors and companions on fishing and hunting trips.

Buster and Barney, both came back to Ole Miss last year, Barney from West Point and 32-year-old Buster after retiring from the New York Giants. One of Buster's chief chores was making a more aggressive, crashing-type end out of the ex-Academy ace.

"I don't say they taught him wrong at West Point," explains Buster. "I just wanted to make him as good defensively as on offense. I think he's proved he can be both."

The Pooles have practically no interests outside the athletic world and their homes: they simply branch off into different kinds of sports. Barney is the most ardent angler and hunter of them all. "Spend every free hour I can in the woods," he

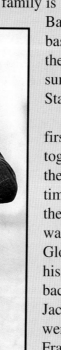

Barney Poole played seven seasons of college football.

declares. Ray, who is 27 and single, plays baseball during the summer. Last season, he pitched the Memphis Chicks with the Southern Association.

In fact, the whole family is "dern good" on the diamond. Barney catches for the Ole Miss baseball team and Buster was on the Rebel nine and played three summers in the Class D Cotton States League.

After all, baseball was their first love, and they still get together occasionally to play on the same squad. The last such time, was a few weeks before they trooped off to grid wars. It was during a big Poole reunion in Gloster. There was Barney and his bride, Buster with his family, bachelor Ray; Flemin, Phillip, Jackie and Leslie. Also around were Leslie's young brothers, Frank, 18; Shirley, 16, and Conway, 14. They're high school stars already in line for athletic scholarships at guess where?

The proud Gloster townspeople took note of the reunion and arranged a celebration, as they often do for the Poole boys.

The feature of the most recent affair was the ball game between an all-Poole nine and a Plaquemin, La., city club. The Pooles won, but nobody remembers the score. Anyway, it was like old times:

A Poole pitching, a Poole catching and Pooles all over the place.

Ole Miss 49   Mississippi State 7

Showboat Boykin's 7 TD's Rout Bulldogs in Egg Bowl

It had never happened before in Ole Miss or Southeastern Conference history. But today, Laverne (Showboat) Boykin, a senior halfback from Greenville, Miss., ripped the Bulldogs for seven touchdowns and led a 49-7 rout over the Rebels cross-state rival.

Boykin's memorable afternoon shattered the SEC's one-game scoring record by 12 points, which had been been set earlier by Kentucky's Bob Davis, who scored 30 points in the mid-1930's.

He scored three touchdowns in the first quarter, one in the second, one in the third and two in the final quarter. Jimmy Lear, from Greenwood, Miss., added the extra-point kick after each of Boykin's end zone journeys.

No one in the crowd of 28,000 had anticipated such an offensive fireworks display.

But Boykin got started early and by the end of the first quarter the Maroons were hanging on by a thread.

Ole Miss advanced the opening kickoff to the Rebel 43. In six plays,

Ole Miss	21	7	7	14	— 49
Mississippi State	0	7	0	0	— 7

they were in the Maroon end zone, with Boykin racing the final 21 yards up the middle for the touchdown.

Boykin's dominance continued.

After Reggie Ott pulled in a Lear pass and carried it to the State 14, Boykin rammed the remaining distance for the touchdown.

Ken Barfield recovered Joe Fortunato's fumble on the next series at the State 25. Lear then passed to Lindy Callahan to move the Rebs to the State 12. One play later, Boykin danced in for touchdown No. 3.

State mounted a brief change in momentum when they ditched their normal split T attack for the single wing. Bill Stewart, State's fullback, capped the touchdown drive on a 5-yard off-tackle blast.

Boykin then picked up where he left off.

The Rebs marched 75 yards in nine plays, with Allen Muirhead's 29-

yard sprint doing most of the damage. Boykin slammed at left guard for 14 yards for touchdown No. 4.

Boykin's next touchdown was a 85-yard sprint down the east sideline to the State end zone in the third quarter. A key block by Callahan cleared up some difficult traffic along the way.

Boykin almost got TD No. 6 when the Rebs advanced to the State 1. A penalty kept them out of the end zone.

But with Muirhead, Lear and Rocky Byrd moving the Rebs to the State 1 again, Boykin got the SEC record with his sixth TD.

A Russ Palton interception of a Wally Beach pass put the Rebs at the State 5. Boykin ran past the dreary Bulldogs for touchdown No. 7 with less than a minute left in the game.

Showboat Boykin Steals Show

Laverne (Showboat) Boykin set a new Southeastern Conference one-game scoring record today by scoring seven touchdowns against Mississippi State.

Here's how the Rebel fullback made his touchdowns:

First Quarter

1. By running 21 yards up the middle.
2. By bowling over just about everybody from 14 yards out.
3. By bulling 12 yards up the center.

Second Quarter

4. By cracking left guard for 14 yards.

Third Quarter

5. By ripping through right guard and up sideline for 85 yards.

Fourth Quarter

6. By socking over from the State 1.
   (this one broke the old SEC record).
7. By plunging five yards through middle.

THE VAUGHT ERA

Showboat Boykin's 7 TD's set a new SEC scoring record.

Ole Miss 21   Maryland 14

November 15, 1952 | Oxford, Miss.

Magnificent Rebels Stop Maryland Win Streak

John Vaught's Rebels made a name for themselves today when they sunk No. 3-ranked Maryland, 21-14, today at Hemingway Stadium. The Rebs' win halted Maryland's 22-game win streak. Jim Tatum, the Maryland coach, said after the contest, "Ole Miss wanted it worse than we did. We wanted it only in our heads, not our hearts. They beat us with our own plays — and they deserved it."

A sellout crowd of 32,500 would agree.

Wilson Dillard was the hero for Ole Miss when he scored a pair of fourth-quarter touchdowns.

The Rebs were halted inside the Maryland 5 on four other occasions.

The win over the 1952 Sugar Bowl champions earned Ole Miss an invitation to the Sugar Bowl on New Year's Day 1953.

The Terrapins scored first at the beginning of the second quarter when Chet Hanulak raced over on a sweep around end. The point-after kick was successful.

Ole Miss matched this on an 83-yard, 13-play drive, which Bud

Maryland	0	14	0	0 —	14
Ole Miss	0	7	0	14 —	21

Howell capped on a touchdown dart.

With the score at 7-all, Dick Nolan took the Rebs' kickoff and sprinted 90 yards to put Maryland ahead, 14-7.

This should have sealed Ole Miss' fate, but the Rebs hadn't been reading the Terps' headlines.

The Rebs were denied the Maryland end zone once in the second quarter and twice in the third but soon took control of the game's momentum.

Jimmy Lear set up a touchdown when he passed to Bud Slay. Dillard bolted over left guard for the touchdown and Lear's extra-point kick evened the score at 14-all.

Maryland, led by all-American quarterback Jack Scarbath, tried to get the Terps moving from the Maryland 38. He fired a 50-yarder to tall

42

THE VAUGHT ERA

Wilson Dillard rams through the Maryland defense for 3 yards en route to the Rebels' third touchdown in the 21-14 win.

Jimmy Lear's long-distance pass to Bud Howell capped an 83-yard, 13-play scoring drive for the Rebels.

THE
VAUGHT
ERA

44

end, Lou Weidensahl, who pulled it out of the hands of Ole Miss defender Jimmy Patton. But the play was nullified by a lineman downfield.

This setback put the Terps into a slide.

The Rebs eventually got the ball back at their 48. Two plays later, Lear flung one deep to Slay who caught it at the Terps' 2. Dillard scored two plays later to put Ole Miss ahead for good, 20-14. Lear's extra-point kick made it 21-14.

Lear won the battle of the quarterbacks with a performance of 11 completions on 16 attempts for 231 yards and rushed for 50 yards. Scarbath, however, had a difficult afternoon — going 59 minutes before completing a pass.

Ole Miss rushed and passed for 461 yards against the No. 1 defense in the country. They also held the No. 4 offense in the country to only 12 yards.

Maryland's offense completed only one pass and crossed midfield only on their second-quarter scoring drive.

THE VAUGHT ERA

Ole Miss 14   Texas Christian 13

January 2, 1956 | Dallas, Tex.

THE VAUGHT ERA

Day Rallies Rebs' Comeback Against TCU Horned Frogs

After falling behind, 13-7, Eagle Day & Co. rebounded in one of the Cotton Bowl's great comebacks to defeat the TCU Horned Frogs, 14-13.It took less than five minutes and was filled with great courage.

With time ticking away, the Rebels marched from their 34 and reached the TCU 29. Day, attempting to pass, couldn't find a receiver, so he pulled the ball down and raced to the TCU 5. Billy Lott veered off right end at a full gallop and crossed the goal line easily to even the score at 13-all. Paige Cothren's point-after kick put the Rebs ahead for good.

The great Horned Frog back, Jim Swink, tried to get TCU back in scoring position, but Eddie Crawford ended their hopes when he intercepted a Frog pass.

A poll of the sportswriters in the Cotton Bowl press box had made TCU the pre-game favorite by a 35-4 margin.

The game had been billed as a duel between the passing prowess of Day and the difficult-to-stop running of Swink.

Ole Miss	0	7	0	7	—	14
Texas Christian	7	6	0	0	—	13

The Frogs lived up to their billing in the first quarter by driving 72 yards for the opening touchdown. Swink dove over from the left side of the Reb 1 to ice the six points. Hal Pollard booted the extra-point kick to make it 7-0.

The Rebs tried to counter when Eddie Crawford swept around end on a pitchout for 60 yards to the TCU end zone, but the play was called back on a holding call against Ole Miss.

In the second quarter, Swink broke off-tackle for 40 yards to put the Frogs ahead, 13-0. Pollard, the Frogs' backup fullback, booted the extra-point kick. However, an offside call against TCU nullified the point. A second try was unsuccessful.

Ole Miss got back in the game on a 4-play drive that traveled 66 yards. Cothren carried for 24 yards on the final two plays to narrow the

The 1955 Rebels posted a record of 10 wins and one loss and were named Southeastern Conference champions.

THE
VAUGHT
ERA

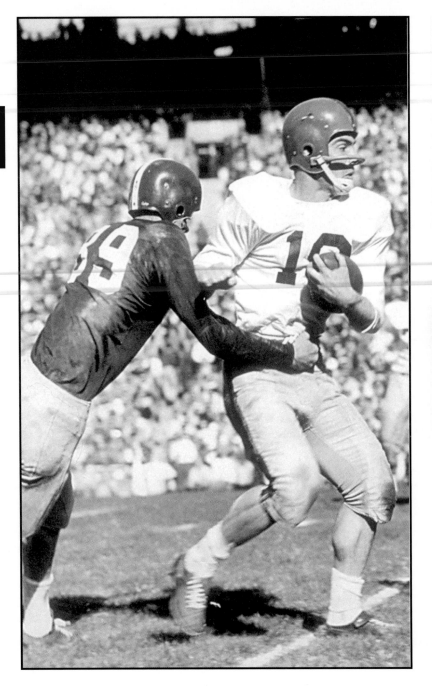

Top: Paige Cothren kicks the winning extra point against the Frogs. Left: Eagle Day tries to elude a TCU tackler.

Frogs' lead to 13-6. Cothren's extra-point kick brought the score to 13-7.

Billy Kinard's pass-catching and Cothren's running brought the Rebs to the TCU 7 before halftime, but the Frog defense stopped a pass in the end zone as the clock ran out.

The second half was a seesaw until the Rebs came to life with less than 5 minutes remaining.

The Frogs rushed for 233 yards and Ole Miss got only 92.

Jim Swink (23) cuts upfield on his 37-yard touchdown run in the second quarter against the Rebels.

THE
VAUGHT
ERA

Ole Miss 39   Texas 7

January 1, 1958 | New Orleans, La.

Brown & Rebs Rout Texans in Sugar Bowl

Ray Brown, the boy wonder from Greenville, Miss., ran for a pair of touchdowns and routed the newly-revived Longhorns, 39-7, in the 24th Sugar Bowl. With the Rebels up, 26-7, in the fourth quarter, many in the crowd of 79,000 began to head for the exits. But the show was just getting exciting.

Brown, who was standing in his end zone ready to punt, when he noticed something he didn't like.

"That big Texas right tackle was coming in too fast. So I ran," Brown later told the press in the Reb locker room.

He then cut left and ran through the grasps of two Texas tacklers near the west sidelines. At the 40 he picked up some blue-shirted blockers. After passing midfield, he was in the clear. An escort of three teammates, two coaches and several Ole Miss cheerleaders trailed him on his journey to the Texas end zone. The actual trip took 103 yards but counted only 92 yards in the record book.

Brown was awarded The Miller-Digby Trophy as the game's most valuable player. He was a unanimous choice — the first ever in Sugar

| Ole Miss | 6 | 13 | 7 | 13 — 39 |
| Texas | 0 | 0 | 0 | 7 — 7 |

Bowl history. His two touchdowns — which matched a Sugar Bowl record, one passing touchdown, three passes intercepted and a touchdown-saving tackle — made him the obvious candidate.

Ole Miss scored in every quarter of the game. Brown dove in from the Texas 1; Don Williams on a pass from Brown; Kent Lovelace on a nine-yard dash around end; Bobby Franklin on a dive from the Texas 3; Brown on his memorable 92-yard run, and Tommy Taylor on a Billy Brewer pass. Bobby Khayat booted three of the extra-point kicks.

Texas opened the game using an unbalanced line with the center on the outside and seemed to make progress early by driving to the Reb 22, but their drive stalled there.

Ken Kirk recovered a Rene Ramirez fumble at the Texas 34. A roughing penalty against Texas moved the ball to the 19. On a series of rollouts against the slow Texas ends, the Rebs moved to the Texas 1. Brown

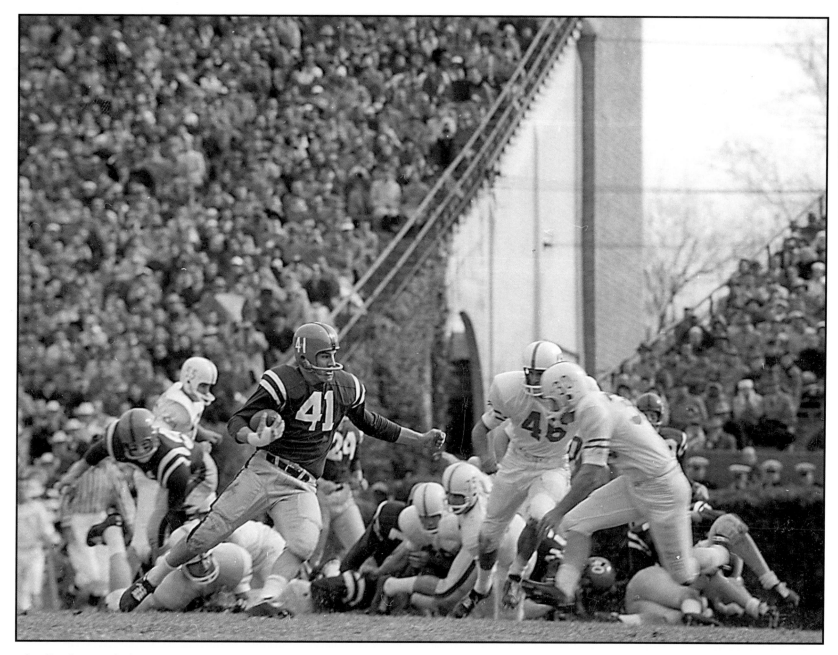

Charlie Flowers (41) sweeps outside against a pair of Texas defenders.

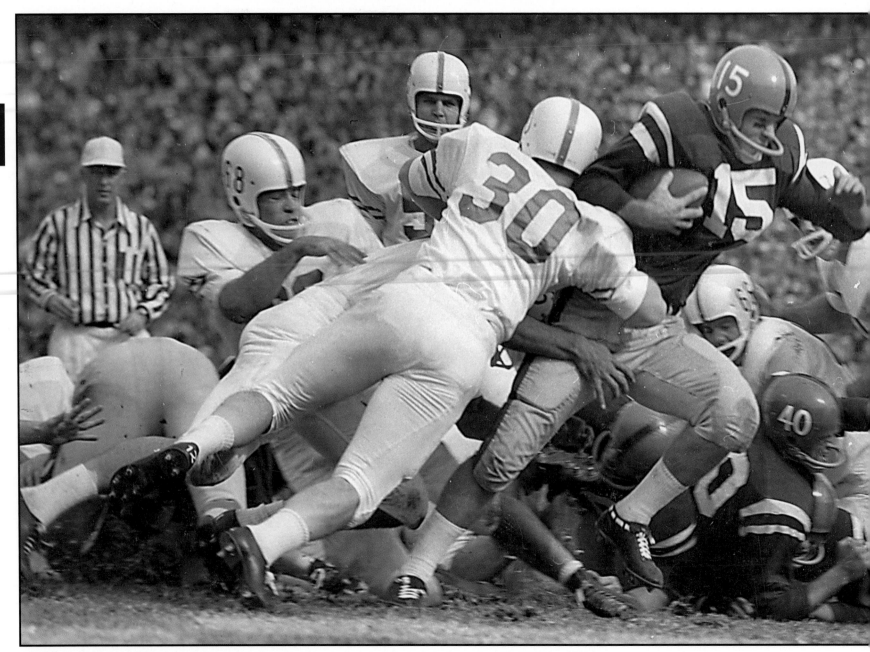

Ray Brown's 92-yard fake-punt romp in the 4th quarter earned him the Sugar Bowl's MVP trophy.

carried over right guard for the touchdown.

Brown finished the day with 157 yards rushing on 15 carries, connected on three passes for 24 yards and 1 TD and punted for an average of 34.7 yards.

A series of rollouts by the Rebels moved the ball 55 yards at the end of the first quarter and at the start of the second. A Brown pass to Williams in the corner of the end zone gave Ole Miss its second TD. Khayat booted the extra point to increase Ole Miss' lead to 13-0.

On the kickoff, George Blanch gathered in Jackie Simpson's kickoff at the Texas 10 and sprinted up the middle of the field. At midfield, only Brown stood in his way and he nailed him. Texas drove to the Reb 18 but a failed Walter Fondren pass ended the Longhorns' hopes.

Ole Miss added to Texas' misery when the Ole Miss defense rushed Bobby Lackey at his 8-yard line, forcing him to throw a bad pass which was intercepted by Brown at the Longhorn 35 and returned to the 20. A series of pitchouts moved the Rebs to the Texas 9. Lovelace then swept end for the 9-yard touchdown run.

Ole Miss led, 19-0, at halftime.

Larry Grantham recovered a Fondren fumble at the Ole Miss 47. Franklin ran for 44 yards and passed 14 yards to Jimmy Hall for the touchdown. Khayat's extra-point kick made it 26-0.

Max Alvis rushed for 2 yards at the beginning of the fourth quarter to narrow the Rebs' lead. Bobby Lackey's kick made it 26-7.

Minutes later, Brown brought the crowd to their feet with his heroics. Then third-team quarterback Billy Brewer passed to Taylor for the final TD.

53

Ole Miss 3   Louisiana State 7

October 31, 1959 | Baton Rouge, La.

Cannon's 89-Yard TD Sprint Dooms Rebs on Halloween

Billy Cannon, LSU's amazing halfback, sprinted 89 yards into history tonight against Ole Miss. It was an unforgettable sight that mesmerized 67,500 fans in Tiger Stadium. Ole Miss had built a 3-0 lead on Bob Khayat's 22-yard field goal before Cannon set out on his game-winning, fourth-quarter run.

To ensure that Cannon's efforts were not in vain, the LSU defense stopped a 59-yard Ole Miss drive led by Doug Elmore on the Tiger 1 in the game's final seconds.

Tiger Stadium erupted when the brilliant LSU defense had Elmore in its grasp.

But it was Cannon's remarkable journey down the sideline that brought life to a Tiger offensive attack that had been unproductive all evening. The Rebels, led by Bobby Franklin and Jake Gibbs, had been punting the ball — including several on first down — in an attempt to keep LSU bottled up, knowing that the Tigers probably couldn't mount an attack to make move the ball.

Ole Miss	3	0	0	0 —	3
Louisiana State	0	0	0	7 —	7

On this occasion, Gibbs, the Rebel quarterback, punted from his 42 on third down. The booming punt traveled 47 yards toward the southeast corner of the field, near the LSU 10-yard line.

Cannon did not try to catch the punt, watching instead as it hit the ground. It then bounced in his direction and he gathered it in at the Tiger 11.

A trio of Rebels got a hand on Cannon but he burst through their grasp as he headed upfield.

Four Ole Miss players stood ahead of Cannon and two of them were directly in his path. Cannon switched toward the east sideline, running past a screaming John Vaught.

When he passed the Reb 40, Cannon was in the clear and the bedlam in Tiger Stadium could have been heard in New Orleans.

Billy Cannon (20) sprints through the Ole Miss defense en route to an 89-yard game-winning touchdown in the 4th quarter.

After Cannon crossed the Rebels' goal line, Tiger Stadium went wild. Wendell Harris booted the extra-point kick which gave LSU a 7-3 lead.

Ole Miss' hopes were left stranded near midfield. But Vaught's troops gathered to make one final valiant effort.

With Elmore, the Rebs' fourth-team quarterback at the helm, Ole Miss gathered in the kickoff and set off on a 15-play drive to retake the lead. With Bobby Crespino, Jim Anderson and Cowboy Woodruff carrying the load and Elmore's big plays, the Rebs marched to the LSU 1.

On the final play of the game, Elmore dove for the game-winning touchdown, but he was met by the entire right half of the Tiger defense, led by Donnie Daye. Elmore was stopped just short of the goal line.

In a bit of irony, it was an earlier Daye fumble that had given the Rebs the ball.

The Ole Miss scoring drive was set up by a Cannon fumble at the LSU 21 after Cannon had traveled 15 yards on the carry. Billy Brewer made the recovery.

Charlie Flowers carried twice to the Tiger 8. Three more runs advanced the ball to the Tiger 5. Khayat then came in and booted the 3-pointer that gave Ole Miss the lead, at 7:25 in the first quarter.

This score stood until the final five minutes of the contest when Cannon went wild.

Ole Miss' 1959 backfield:
(top to bottom)
**Bobby Franklin, George Blair,
Charlie Flowers and Bobby Crespino.**

Ole Miss 21   Louisiana State 0

January 1, 1960 | New Orleans, La.

Franklin's Passing Hobbles LSU in Rematch

Today's Sugar Bowl proved once again that you should never get greedy.

After a thrilling and near-miraculous 7-3 win over Ole Miss on Halloween night, LSU should have settled for the victory over a SEC foe. Instead, Ole Miss came to play with revenge on their mind and plastered the Tigers, 21-0, before a crowd of 81,500 in this Dixie rematch.

Ole Miss scored all three touchdowns on passes.

Jake Gibbs unleashed a 42-yarder to James (Cowboy) Woodruff in the second quarter for the Rebs' first touchdown. Bobby Franklin threw the other two — to Larry Grantham for 18 yards in the third quarter and to George Blair for nine yards in the fourth quarter. Franklin booted one of the extra points. Bobby Khayat added the other two.

Franklin was awarded The Miller-Digby Trophy as the game's most valuable player after the final buzzer.

Across the field, Billy Cannon, who had stolen Ole Miss' thunder — and perhaps victory — with his 89-yard gallop on Halloween night, was

| Ole Miss | 0 | 7 | 7 | 7 — | 21 |
| LSU | 0 | 0 | 0 | 0 — | 0 |

57

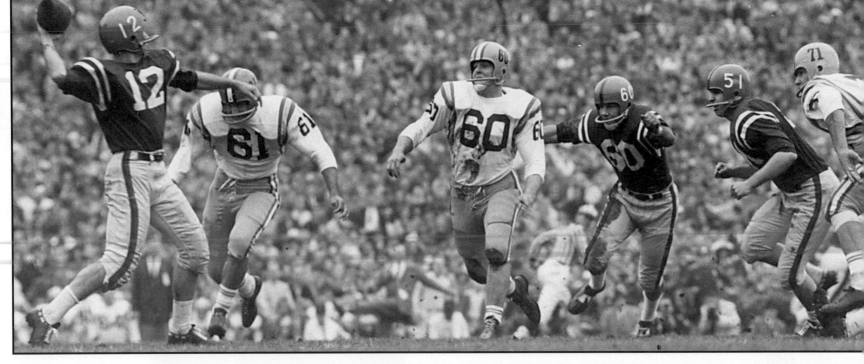

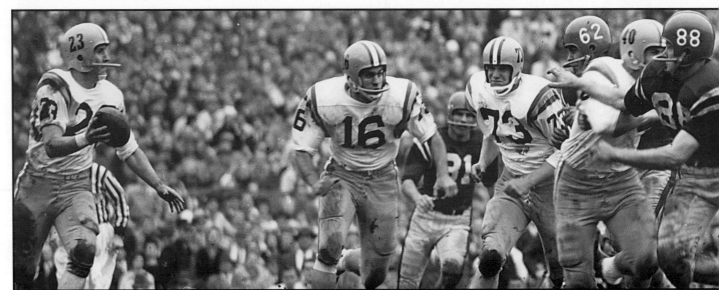

Top: Jake Gibbs (12) passes to Cowboy Woodruff for a 43-yard touchdown in the 1st half.

Right: The stingy Ole Miss defense held LSU scoreless in their famed rematch.

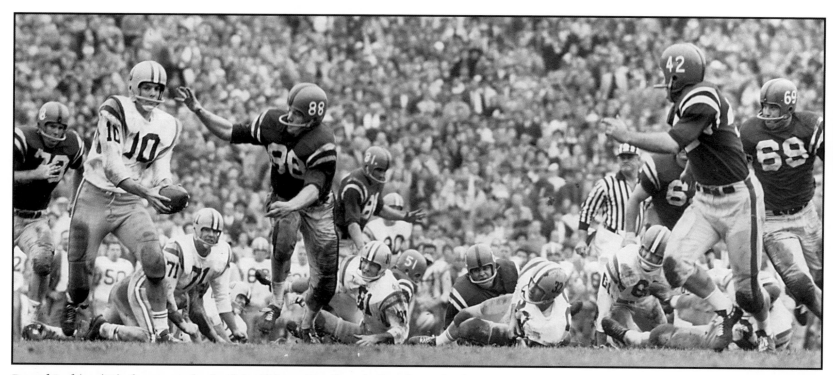

Darryl Jenkins (10), the quarterback of the Chinese Bandits, eluding the rush of Larry Grantham (88), looks for an opening in the Rebel defense.

THE VAUGHT ERA

only able to muster eight yards on the ground. The Ole Miss defense went everywhere with him on the field. It was a frustrating afternoon for the great all-American halfback.

LSU lost 15 yards on the ground and gained only 89 yards in the air.

It took the Tigers 51 minutes and 45 seconds before they crossed midfield and into Ole Miss territory.

The Rebs, however, moved the ball to the LSU 20 the first time they got the ball. The drive ended in an interception.

At the beginning of the second quarter, the Rebs drove to the LSU 16. Khayat's missed field goal stopped that one.

Another drive to the LSU 11 ended in frustration, too.

Then, just before halftime, Gibbs piloted the Rebels to gloryland, hitting Woodruff on a 42-yard pass that finished in the Tiger end zone.

Franklin booted the point-after kick to put Ole Miss up, 7-0.

After intermission, Franklin led the Rebs on a 64-yard, 9-play march to the LSU goal line. An 18-yard pass to Grantham ended in a touchdown.

In the final quarter, Franklin guided the Rebs on a 75-yard drive to paydirt. Three passes covered the last 44 yards, with Blair grabbing a 9-yard pass for the touchdown.

Durel Matherne, the quarterback of the Go team, led the Tigers on their first penetration into Ole Miss territory. The drive would reach the Reb 34 before James Anderson sacked Matherne for a 19-yard loss while attempting to pass.

The LSU fans were so upset after the loss they forgot to visit the French Quarters.

Ole Miss 10   Arkansas 7

October 22, 1960 | Little Rock, Ark.

Green's 4th Quarter Kick Defeats Porkers

The clock on the scoreboard in the end zone showed three seconds remaining. The center's snap passed the ball to the holder, Jake Gibbs, and Ole Miss kicker Allen Green booted the most important field goal of the season. It traveled 39 yards and passed through the uprights as the final buzzer sounded to give the Rebs a 10-7 victory.

For Green and Ole Miss this is what heaven must be like.

For Porker fans, there would be no celebration in the capital city.

This was Green's second try at the game-winning kick. He had made an attempt with 16 seconds left, but an official's time-out had nullified the kick.

Arkansas had scored on a 67-yard, 12-play drive on a George McKinney pass to Jimmy Gaston in the second quarter. Mickey Cissell's extra-point kick made it 7-0.

Ole Miss, however, bounced back after halftime with a 57-yard bomb from Gibbs to Ralph Smith. Green booted the extra-point kick that tied the game at 7-all.

Ole Miss	0	0	7	3 —	10
Arkansas	0	7	0	0 —	7

The Porkers almost broke the tie when Cissell, a sophomore from Wilson, Ark., attempted a field goal midway of the fourth quarter, but it fell short.

Gibbs & Co. then marched from their 25 to the game-winning field goal.

Arkansas entered the game with only one loss. Curtis Cox and Lance Alworth, an all-America from Brookhaven, Miss., kept the Reb defense busy all afternoon.

Following the game, Arkansas coach Frank Broyles questioned referee Thomas Bell's call on the final field goal, saying it was wide of the mark.

THE VAUGHT ERA

Jake Gibbs (12) passes 57 yards to Ralph Smith to tie the game at 7-7 in the third quarter.

Ole Miss 14   Rice 6

January 2, 1961 | New Orleans, La.

THE VAUGHT ERA

Gibbs Sparks No. 1 Rebs to Victory Over Rice

Jake Gibbs stood tall when Ole Miss needed him against the Rice Owls and the Grenada field general delivered a 14-6 win in the 27th Sugar Bowl. The victory earned them a No. 1 ranking in the Football Writers of America poll.

Gibbs scored twice for the Rebs — in the first quarter and later in the final quarter. It was the only time Ole Miss crossed the Rice goal line all afternoon. Allen Green booted both of the Ole Miss point-after kicks.

Rice had to play lots of defense to slow down the Rebels. The Owls finally got on the scoreboard in the third quarter when Butch Blume dashed into the corner of the end zone to narrow the score at 7-6. Max Webb's extra-point kick was wide.

82,851 packed Tulane Stadium for this gridiron chess match.

Gibbs' outstanding play earned him The Miller-Digby Trophy as the game's most valuable player. He completed just 5 of 15 passes for 43 yards but groundout key yardage when necessary for the Rebs, including more than 40 yards in the fourth-quarter scoring drive.

Ole Miss	7	0	0	7 —	14
Rice	0	0	6	0 —	6

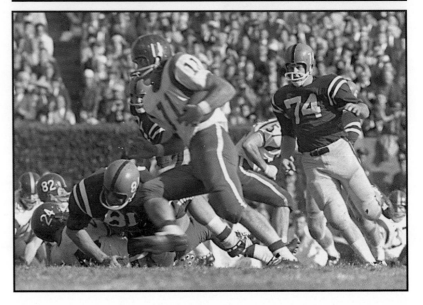

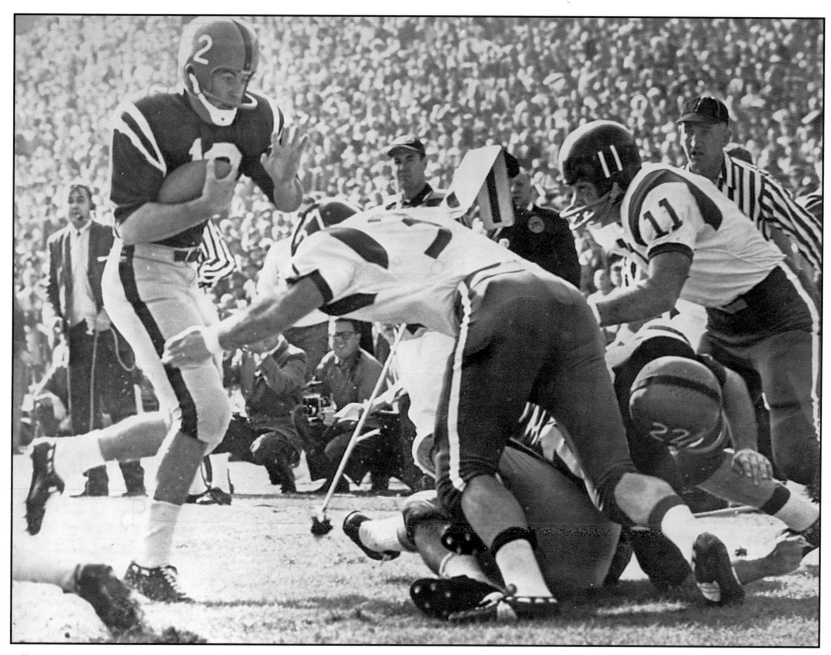

THE
VAUGHT
ERA

All-American quarterback Jake Gibbs (12) scored on a 15-yard sprint during the game's opening drive.

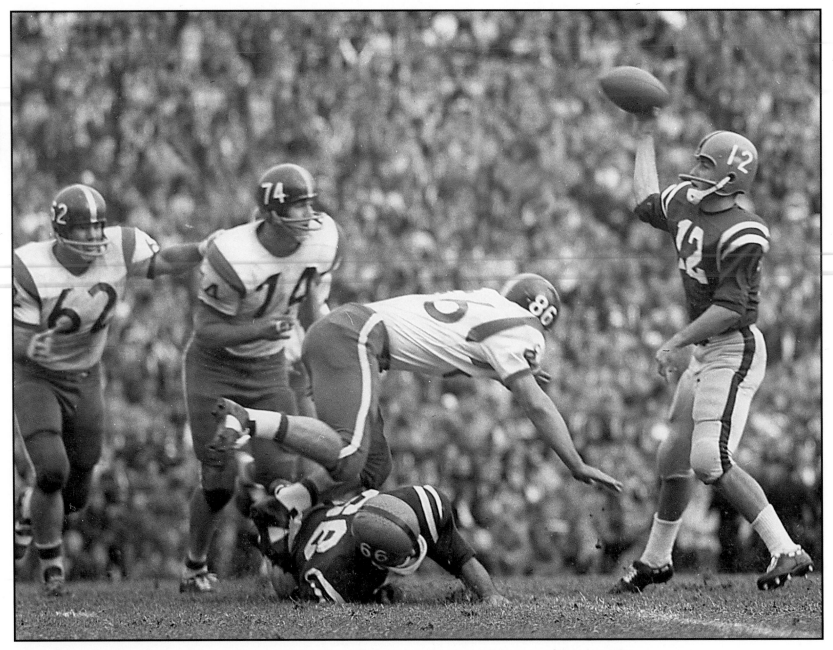

Jake Gibbs (12) completed only five of 15 passes for 43 yards, but scored two touchdowns on the ground.

Jake Gibbs was named MVP.

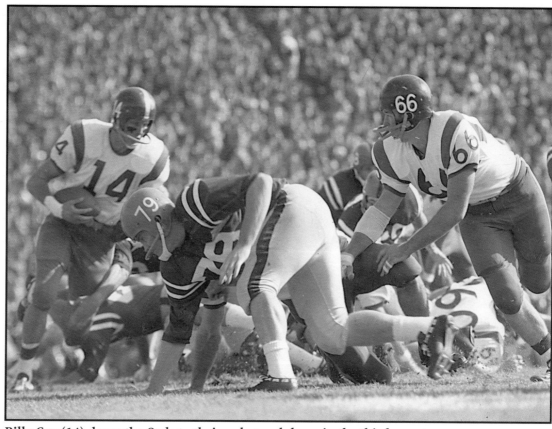

Billy Cox (14) drove the Owls to their only touchdown in the third quarter.

THE
VAUGHT
ERA

At times, it seemed as if the Rice defense was short of players. After advancing the opening kickoff to their 35, Gibbs' crew churned up 65 yards in seven plays for the touchdown. Bobby Crespino ate up 15 yards on a reverse around end on the longest play of the drive.

The Rebs drove to the Rice 32 on their next drive before losing the ball.

Rice got their offense moving in the second quarter by traveling to the Reb 31, the Reb 9 and the Reb 18. All three drives were stopped by Reb interceptions.

Rice took the second-half kickoff and marched to the Reb 22. Webb's failed field goal ended the drive.

In the third quarter, the Owls drove 77 yards on 18 plays to reach the Rebs' goal line. Billy Cox threw four passes on the Owls' march. Blume wrapped up the six points on a 2-yard burst.

Jim Anderson, Art Doty and Gibbs then began their final scoring drive by pounding on the right side of the Rice line.

Gibbs ripped for the touchdown to put Ole Miss ahead, 13-6. Green's kick made it 14-6.

65

Ole Miss 17   Arkansas 13

January 1, 1963 | New Orleans, La.

Griffing Passes Rebs Past Arkansas In Sugar Bowl

Glynn Griffing led Ole Miss to a 17-13 lead against Arkansas in the 29th Sugar Bowl and then fought to hold onto victory.

For his efforts, Griffing was voted The Miller-Digby Trophy as the game's most valuable player. He connected on 14 of 23 passes for 242 yards and broke the Sugar Bowl passing record set by TCU's Davey O'Brien in 1939 against Carnegie Tech. O'Brien's record had been 235.

Ole Miss scored first by driving from its 20 to the Arkansas 13. When the Porkers' defense stiffened, Billy Carl Irwin booted a 30-yard field goal.

This was matched by the Porkers' Tom McKnelly's 20-yard field goal to tie the score at 3-3. The drive began with Billy Gray passing deep to Jerry Lamb at midfield. Lamb grabbed the catch and sprinted to the Ole Miss 13 before Buck Randall tripped him up. The play traveled 67 yards.

The Rebs responded with Griffing flinging a 33-yard pass to Louis Guy for a touchdown. Irwin's extra-point kick made it 10-3.

Ole Miss	0	10	7	0 —	17
Arkansas	0	3	10	0 —	13

In the third quarter, Arkansas' Ray Trail recovered a Buck Randall fumble at the Ole Miss 18. The Porkers then wasted no time in finding the Rebel end zone. Billy Moore passed to Jesse Branch for a five-yard touchdown pass. McKnelly added the point-after kick to tie the score at 10-all.

Griffing then marched his Rebs 80 yards to break the ice. Griffing dove for the touchdown and Irwin kicked the point-after to put Ole Miss ahead, 17-10.

The Rebs' touchdown caused the Porkers to see red.

Arkansas roared downfield to the Ole Miss 5, aided by a memorable Gray to Jerry Lamb pass. When the Rebs held, McKnelly kicked a 22-yard field goal to narrow the Rebs' lead to 17-13 with 1:33 left in the third quarter.

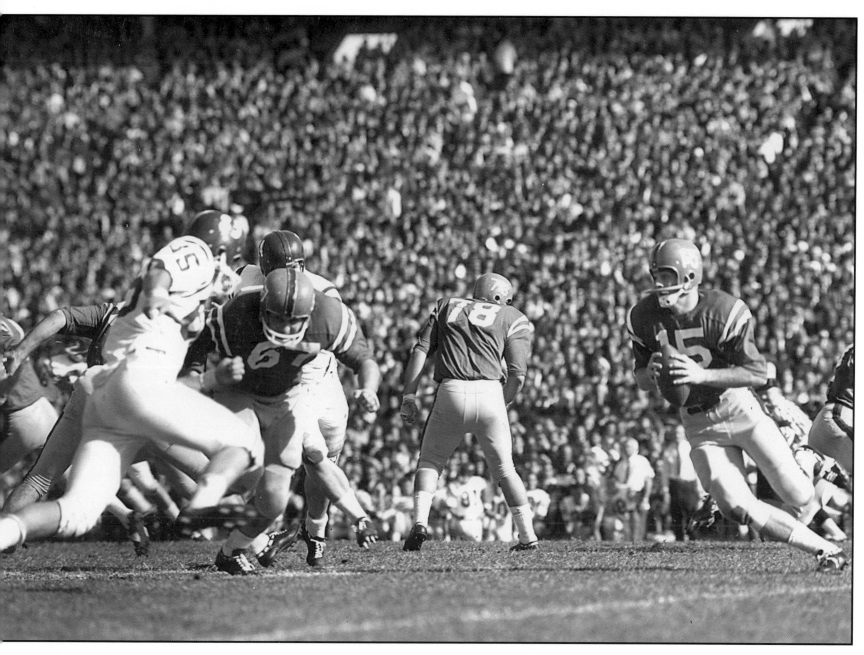

THE VAUGHT ERA

Glynn Griffing (15) was named the game's MVP after he rushed for 41 yards and passed for 242 yards.

Tommy More (45) boomed a 60-yard punt that pushed the Rebs deep into their territory.

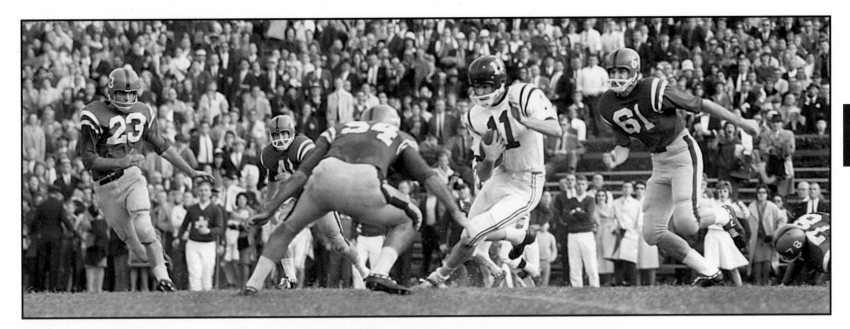

THE VAUGHT ERA

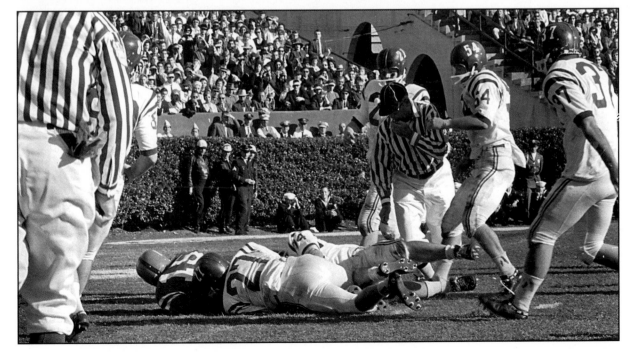

The Porkers kept trying to find the Ole Miss end zone until Fred Kimbrell intercepted a Gray pass with less than one minute left in the contest.

Guy finished the afternoon with 107 yards on five catches — all from Griffing.

Top: Bill Gray (11), the Arkansas quarterback, gained 11 yards to move the ball to the Ole Miss 22.

Bottom: Glynn Griffing dives for a touchdown to put the Rebels ahead, 17-10.

69

Everyone Agrees on Griffing

By Carl P. Leubsdorf

The Associated Press

THE
VAUGHT
ERA

NEW ORLEANS — Mississippi's Glynn Griffing, "the best passer I've ever seen," was the difference in today's Sugar Bowl football game, Arkansas coach Frank Broyles said in the dressing room following the contest.

Griffing's running and passing, which set a Sugar Bowl record of 242 yards on 14 completions, led Ole Miss to a 17-13 victory over the Razorbacks.

"It was those big third-down plays when he would get away from us and complete the pass that was the difference," Broyles said. "He's the greatest college quarterback in America. In fact, he's the best college passer I've ever seen."

Griffing, who was named the outstanding player in the Sugar Bowl, signed a professional contract with the New York Giants of the National Football League. He was drafted by them as a junior after the 1961 season.

Arkansas coach Frank
Broyles called Glynn
Griffing "The best college
passer I've ever seen."

70

Ole Miss' Quarterbacks Shine in Sugar Bowl

Reb quarterback Ray Brown

Ole Miss is Quarterback U.

And when they arrive in the Sugar Bowl they usually leave with a victory notched in their belt.

Glynn Griffing was the star pupil this afternoon in Tulane Stadium. Ray Brown had the role of the Rebs' brilliant field general in 1958. Bobby Franklin had that role in 1960. The next year it was Jake Gibbs.

John Vaught's quarterbacks know how to shine while in the Crescent City. Brown ran and passed for three touchdowns, including an unforgettable 92-yard run and intercepted a record three passes, as the Rebels beat Texas, 39-7. Franklin threw for 148 yards on 10 completions as the Rebs got revenge against LSU in a 21-0 shutout. Gibbs scored both of Ole Miss' touchdowns in a 14-6 win over Rice.

Griffing's heroics put him in the spotlight. He passed for 242 yards and rushed for 41 yards against the Porkers. His passing mark broke the record that Davey O'Brien set against Carnegie Tech in 1939.

Following the game, Arkansas coach Frank Broyles noted, "Glynn Griffing is the greatest of all quarterbacks."

Vaught, his coach, added, "There's no doubt about it. Griffing was the difference in the ball game."

Ole Miss 13   Auburn 7

December 18, 1965 | Memphis, Tenn.

Rebs Stop Tiger Rally in Liberty Bowl

John Vaught's stingy, blue-shirted defense pounded Auburn quarterback Alex Bowden at the Reb 16 on fourth down in the game's final seconds to preserve Ole Miss' 13-7 victory in the inaugural Liberty Bowl game in chilly Memphis. The Tigers had driven 55 yards from their 36 to the Reb 9 in a final attempt to wrest away Ole Miss' lead. But with one yard remaining for a first down and only eight yards from the Ole Miss goal, the skinny Bowden was unable to escape the onslaught of the Rebel defense.

Jimmy Keyes, the Reb middle guard, booted the field goals of 42 and 30 yards that ensured the Rebels win.

An Auburn field goal supplied lots of excitement and protest from the Tigers' bench.

Trailing 10-7, Don Lewis booted a field goal from the Reb 21. Kicking from an angle, the ball seemed to have gone high above the goalposts. But the referee, Red Cavette, signaled the ball to be off to the right.

The Auburn holder, Tom Bryan, immediately protested, pointing to

Ole Miss	0	3	7	3 —	13
Auburn	0	7	0	0 —	7

the runway where Lewis' kick had landed. The officials, however, weren't listening to the complaint.

Bryan, the former quarterback who now played fullback was the most valuable player of the game. He led the Tigers in rushing with 111 yards on 18 carries. Mike Dennis and Jimmy Hiedel, the Reb quarterback, had 75 and 72 yards.

Ole Miss had 189 yards rushing and 24 yards passing overall. Auburn rushed for 156 yards and threw for 112 yards, with Bowden completing 11 of 24 attempts.

Following the game, Vaught described the game as "tough. Not outstanding in scoring, but a thriller from start to finish."

He added, "the turning point was when we threw Bowden for a loss in the last minute."

THE
VAUGHT
ERA

Bobby Wade (43) looks for daylight in the Auburn defense while Jerry Richardson (55) stops Auburn's Tom Bryan (19).

Ole Miss 10   Alabama 8

October 5, 1968 | Jackson, Miss.

THE VAUGHT ERA

Rebels Stop Alabama, First Win Since 1910

The drought is over for Ole Miss. After the Rebels defeated Alabama, 10-8, in Mississippi Memorial Stadium, they ended 58 years of frustration. The Rebels' last win against Alabama had been in 1910. "We didn't make a mistake until the fourth quarter," Ole Miss John Vaught explained. "We wanted this one badly."

The mistake Vaught referred to was Alabama linebacker Mike Hall's block of a Julian Fagan punt. Mike Riley recovered the ball in the Reb end zone for an Alabama touchdown with eight seconds left in the game. Joe Kelley passed to fullback Pete Gilleba for the two-point conversion that narrowed Ole Miss' lead to 10-8, but it was too late at that point.

The game was decided by too much Archie Manning, too much Bo Bowen, too much Steve Hindman and too much Rebel defense.

Following the game, Alabama coach Paul (Bear) Bryant made his way to the Ole Miss locker room. Once there, the happy scene got real quiet as Bryant congratulated the Rebel squad.

Alabama	0	0	0	8 —	8
Ole Miss	0	7	3	0 —	10

Seeing Hindman, a tailback, at a nearby locker, Bryant noted, "I'm glad you're a senior." Hindman had rushed for 42 yards in the game.

A crowd of 47,152, the largest ever gathered in Mississippi history, watched this wonderful spectacle take place.

Ole Miss' scoring took place on a pair of explosive series.

Manning, the sophomore from Drew, Miss., with the gifted arm, marched the Rebels 80 yards in five plays. Most of the yardage was covered on a 49-yard pass from Manning to sophomore wingback Vernon Studdard. A personal foul penalty moved the Rebs to the Tide 6. Manning then threw to Hank Snows for the TD. Perry Kings' extra point gave the Rebs a 7-0 lead with barely a minute left in the first half.

King booted a 44-yard field goal in the third quarter to increase that lead to 10-0.

74

THE
VAUGHT
ERA

Tommy Wade (38) tries to corner Ole Miss quarterback Archie Manning before he reaches the Alabama goal line.

Top left: Rebel monsterman Robert Bailey stops Alabama fullback Phil Chaffin (31) from scoring a TD in the first quarter.

Bottom: Roger Crowson (35) and the Tide defense chase after a Don Farrar fumble.

Paul (Bear) Bryant,
left, congratulates John
Vaught after the Rebels'
first win over Alabama
since 1910.

The Ole Miss defense then hung on.

"I didn't think they could score on us," Reb tackle Buz Morrow explained. "I don't think anybody could drive on us."

Except for the fluke touchdown at the end of the game, Alabama didn't get past the Ole Miss 34 in the second half.

Alabama crossed midfield three times in the first half. Twice the Tide attempted field goals — by Oran Buck from the Rebel 38 and 24 — but both attempts failed.

A third threat by the Tide failed when a Kelley pass to Phil Chaffin on fourth down was successful but Bob Bailey tackled him for no gain at the Reb 6. Ole Miss then took over.

THE VAUGHT ERA

Ole Miss 32   Alabama 33

October 4, 1969 | Birmingham, Ala.

Tide Wins Unforgettable Shootout With Ole Miss

In the greatest passing duel ever played in Southeastern Conference history, Alabama held off the feisty Rebels, 33-32 this evening.

The game, which was televised nationally, matched the red-haired bomber from Ole Miss, Archie Manning, and Alabama's aerial artist, Scott Hunter.

Their coaches, Paul (Bear) Bryant of Alabama and John Vaught of Ole Miss, had won six national titles between them. But they had never seen such a fireworks display.

"I've never seen a game like it, not with us in it," Bryant explained after the game while dressing in his locker room.

Later at his hotel room, Vaught shook his head and noted: "I've never had a team to give everything they had into one football game. That's what we did and we were one point short."

Chris Schenkel, who broadcast the game for ABC-TV, added, "It was the most exciting game I've seen in 20 years of broadcasting."

A Legion Field crowd of 62,858 left the game emotionally drained,

Ole Miss	7	0	13	12 —	32
Alabama	7	7	7	12 —	33

still looking back at the empty playing field and the end-zone scoreboards that flashed the final score of 33-32. The millions more who watched the contest on television headed to the refrigerator and then to the couch to relax and ponder about what they had seen.

Manning was amazing. He completed 33 of 52 passes for 426 yards and ran for 104 yards on 15 carries. His efforts totaled 540 yards. He also scored three touchdowns running and two by passing.

His opponent, Hunter, threw 29 passes and completed 22 for 300 yards.

However, it was Alabama's defense that made the difference.

In the second quarter, they forced a pair of game-turning events. First, with 6:39 left before halftime, Tide rover Danny Gilbert pounded Ole Miss end Riley Myers at the Alabama 4, which caused a fumble that

78

THE
VAUGHT
ERA

Rebel quarterback Archie Manning (18) passed for 426 yards and two touchdowns against Alabama.

Bill Blair, Mike Dean (26) and Alex Pittman (58) wrap up Rebel receiver Floyd Franks near the Tide goal line.

**Archie Manning (18)
scores one of his three
TD's against the Tide.**

was recovered by Paul Boschung. Later, with only 35 seconds before intermission, the Tide defense jammed Randy Reed's for a 1-yard loss at the Alabama 9.

In the fourth quarter, the Tide defense stopped Manning on fourth and one at the Alabama 45 after the Reb quarterback bobbled a snap on a quarterback sneak.

The game-winner for Alabama came on the previous series when Alabama drove 80 yards in 11 plays for a touchdown. The drive was capped by a 14-yard pass from Hunter to George Ranager on fourth down and 10.

In the passing duel between Ole Miss' Archie Manning and Alabama's Scott Hunter a total of 24 team, SEC or NCAA records were set or tied.

**THE
VAUGHT
ERA**

Alabama quarterback Scott Hunter completed 22 of 29 passes for 300 yards in the Tide's 33-32 win.

Randy Reed (24) struggles for yardage against the middle of the Tide defense.

THE
VAUGHT
ERA

Archie Manning (18) and Scott Hunter (12) put on the greatest passing display ever seen in the South with 726 yards in total passing.

An Expanded Record Book

NCAA

Two-team, single game offense most passes completed — Manning and Hunter, 55. Previous high 53 by New Mexico (37) and Texas-El Paso (16), 1967; and Brigham Young (32) and Texas-El Paso (21), 1966.

SEC

Pass attempts — Manning, 52. Previous high 49 by Florida's Steve Spurrier vs. Miami, 1966.

Pass Completions — Manning, 33. Previous high 27 by Spurrier vs. Auburn, 1966.

Passing yardage — Manning, 436. Previous high 409 by Florida's John Reaves vs. Houston, 1969.

Total offense — Manning, 540. Previous high 414 by Georgia's Larry Rakestraw vs. Miami, 1963.

Team pass attempts — Ole Mass, 52. Previous high 51 by Florida vs. Miami, 1966.

Team pass completions — Ole Miss, 33. Previous high 29 by Ole Miss vs. Chattanooga, 1947.

Team passing yardage — Ole Miss, 436. Previous high 407 by Georgia vs. Miami, 1950.

Total offensive plays — Manning, 67. Previous high 62 by Manning vs. Southern Mississippi, 1968: and Tennessee's Bubba Wyche vs. Auburn, 1968.

Most Passes without interceptions in a game — Alabama, 30. Previous mark 28 by Florida vs. Florida State, 1965.

OLE MISS

Total first downs — 30. Previous high 28 vs. Florida State, 1961.

Passes completed — Manning, 33. Previous high 24 by Manning vs. LSU, 1968.

Passes attempted — Manning, 52. Previous high 40 by Manning vs. LSU, 1968.

Passing yardage — Manning, 436. Previous high 345 by Manning vs. LSU, 1968.

Team passing yardage — 436. Previous high 351 vs. Houston, 1961.

Total offense — Manning, 540. Previous high 362 by Manning vs. LSU, 1968.

Team passes completed — 33. Previous high 29 vs. Chattanooga, 1947.

Team passes attempted — 52. Previous high 45 vs. Chattanooga, 1947.

First downs passing — 17. Previous high 15 vs. Arkansas, 1952.

Pass reception yardage — 191 by Floyd Franks, Previous high 136 by Leroy Reed vs. LSU, 1956.

Total offense plays — Manning, 67. Previous high 62 by Manning vs. Southern Mississippi, 1968.

TIED — Most passes caught — Franks, 13. Equals Barney Poole vs. Chattanooga, 1947.

ALABAMA

Most passes completed — Hunter, 22. Previous high 19 by Hunter vs. Tennessee, 1968; and Ken Stabler vs. Southern Mississippi, 1967.

Most yards passing — Hunter, 300. Previous high 239 by Hunter vs. Virginia Tech, 1969.

Total offense — Hunter, 303. Previous high 270 by Joe Namath vs. Miami, 1962.

THE
VAUGHT
ERA

85

Ole Miss 26   Louisiana State 23

THE VAUGHT ERA

Manning & Co. End LSU's Unbeaten Streak

Archie Manning made it two in a row against the Bengal Tigers in a 26-23 win over their archrival last season, Manning & Co. defeated LSU, 27-24. The red-headed junior from Drew, Miss., kept the Tiger defense on its heels most of the evening. He ran for three touchdowns, passed for another and completed 22 of 36 passes for 210 yards.

LSU, however, made a fight of the contest. They had the lead at three different times, including a comfortable 23-12 lead in the third quarter.

In the final quarter, they had a chance to win the game, but LSU coach Charles McClendon refused to go for a game-tying field goal and instead opted to cash it in against the Rebs on a pass from LSU quarterback Mike Hillman to Bill Stober, which was knocked out of the receiver's hands in the last moment.

Manning then held the ball as the clock wound down.

Cannon, the Rebs' playmaker on defense, was also a factor in last season's 27-24 win over the Tigers. He intercepted a pass near the end of the game which sealed LSU's fate. In this year's battle, he batted down

LSU	7	9	7	0 —	23
Ole Miss	0	12	14	0 —	26

three Tiger passes in the game's closing minutes.

LSU finished the game with 336 yards of total offense and the Rebels had 278.

The game's lead bounced back and forth several times.

The Rebels' winning drive was a thriller. LSU led, 23-18, in the third quarter and was driving on their 37 when the Ole Miss defense sacked Hillman, forcing him to fumble.

Ole Miss' Larry Thomas recovered the ball at the LSU 23. After a 15-yard penalty for having an ineligible receiver downfield, Manning went to work. He passed to Bo Bowen and Fred Franks and ran on fourth down to move the ball to the LSU 11. A pass to Leon Felts moved the ball to the LSU 1. Manning danced into the end zone untouched on the next play.

Archie Manning (18) passed for 210 yards, ran for 3 touchdowns and passed for another in the 26-23 win over LSU.

Following the game, McClendon, the Tigers coach, recalled, "That was just one of our mistakes. We had too many at the end." Manning cashed in by running for the two-point conversion to give Ole Miss a 26-23 lead. Two previous two-point attempts had failed.

Manning had a hot hand this afternoon. He completed 10 passes in a row at one stretch. Jimbo Poole, a member of the Rebels' greatest football family, caught five of these.

The Rebel quarterback later explained the frantic game-winning drive. "They kept coming at us and fighting off our blockers. It was a good one to win."

LSU scored first in the contest. Tommy Casanova, a great two-way player for the Tigers, intercepted a Manning pass at the Ole Miss 35. Quarterback Jim Gilbert ran it in from the Reb 1 for the touchdown. The extra-point kick gave the Tigers a 7-0 lead.

87

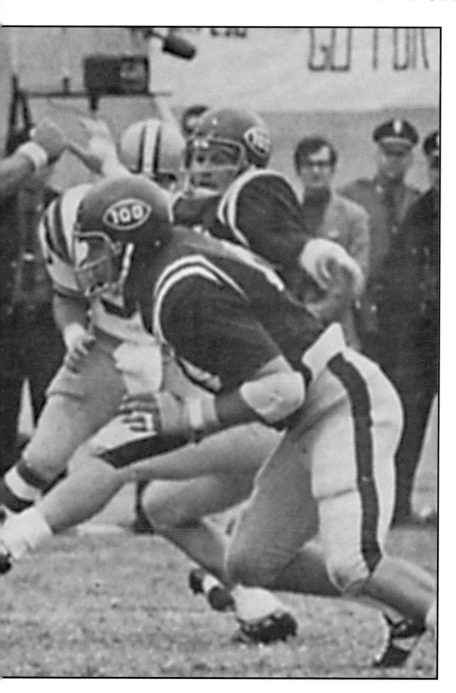

LSU quarterback Mike Hillman (18) holds on to the ball tightly to keep it from being stripped by an Ole Miss defender.

Manning & Co. matched this with a 70-yard drive in the second quarter. Manning ran the final five yards for the touchdown. Perry King missed the extra-point kick, which required the Rebs to attempt the series of two-point plays.

Hillman and Allen Shorey passed and ran to set up the first of three Mark Lumpkin field goals. This one was good from 36 yards.

The Rebs drove 80 yards, with Manning passing to Poole and Franks to cover most of the yardage. Manning passed the final 9 yards to Vernon Studdard, who made a diving catch in the end zone, which put Ole Miss ahead, 12-10.

THE VAUGHT ERA

Ole Miss 38   Tennessee 0

November 15, 1969 | Jackson, Miss.

Manning & Rebs Shutout No. 3-Ranked Vols

John Vaught's football powerhouse scaled the mountaintop of Southeastern Conference football today when they pummeled No. 3-ranked Tennessee, 38-0, in front of a record crowd of 47,220 in Mississippi Memorial Stadium. Vaught later called this game "the greatest effort by an Ole Miss team."

It was the worst defeat of a Tennessee football team since 1923 when Vandy pounded the Vols, 51-7. It was Vol coach Doug Dickey's worst loss since his first season in Knoxville when Ole Miss defeated the Vols, 30-0.

The Rebs' win over Tennessee shook up the bowl picture. The Rebels, 6-3 this season, should be in consideration for a major bowl invitation. They have now defeated traditional powerhouses, Georgia, LSU and Tennessee. Tennessee is 7-1.

The game had been billed as a showdown between Reb quarterback Archie Manning and the Vols' all-American linebacker, Steve Kiner. But the showdown never occurred.

Manning was in control all afternoon. The junior Ole Miss passer

Tennessee	0	0	0	0 —	0
Ole Miss	2	13	7	7 —	38

completed 9 of 18 passes for 159 yards and one touchdown. This gave him a total of 137 completions and 1,946 yards of total offense for the season so far which broke the 22-year-old record set by Charlie Conerly. Conerly had 133 completions and 1,784 yards of total offense in 1947. Manning also topped his own record of 1,510 yards passing last season with 1,553 — and he still has to play the Bulldogs of Mississippi State.

Floyd Franks, the Rebel wingback, caught three passes for 86 yards. This gave him 654 yards for the season, which breaks an earlier record set by Jack Stribling of 598 yards set in 1949. His total of 73 receptions tops the 70 caught by Barney Poole in 1947.

The Vols only crossed into Ole Miss territory three times. In the second quarter they reached the Reb 13. In the third quarter, they were

THE
VAUGHT
ERA

Rebel halfback Randy Reed (24), who rushed for 85 yards on 22 carries, runs into a dead end in the Tennessee defense.

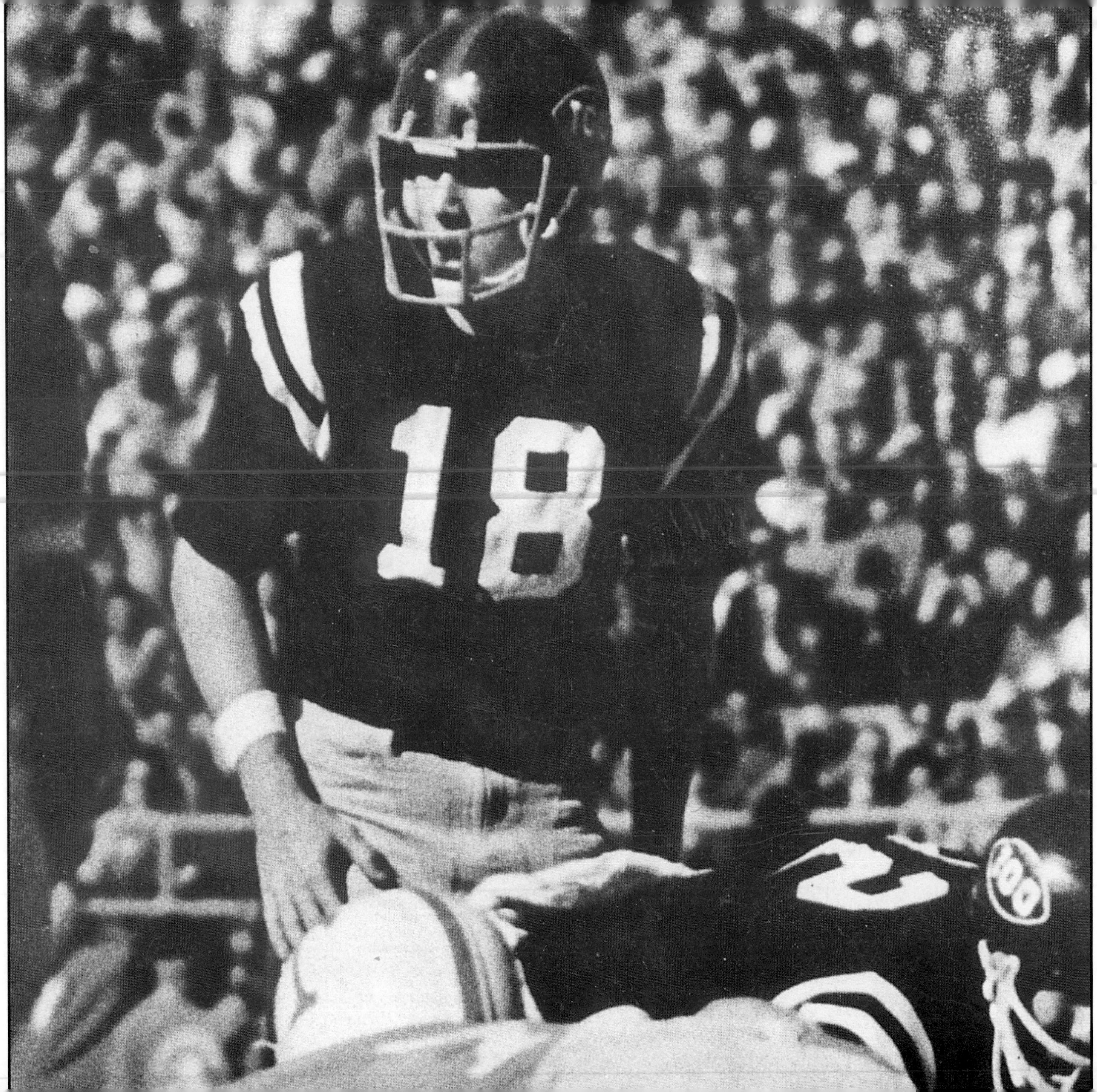

The Rebels' defense upstaged the No. 3-ranked Vols who entered this contest with an undefeated 8-game win streak.

THE VAUGHT ERA

stopped on the Reb 3. In the last quarter Glenn Cannon intercepted a Vol pass at the Reb 5.

The Rebs got on the scoreboard when Manning marched the offense 82 yards in 11 plays. An 11-yard romp by Bo Bowen was a clincher in the drive. Manning carried the ball the final yard for the touchdown with 10:21 left in the first quarter.

Vaught later described the first drive: "We worked on our running game ... and that first series went perfect. Just like we wanted."

Randy Reed rushed for 85 yards on 22 carries this afternoon. Bowen added 104 yards on 19 carries and a touchdown.

The Rebs scored on their next possession when Manning fumbled on a fourth-down touchdown dive that was recovered by Reed in the

Left: Archie Manning (18) broke Charlie Conerly's 22-year-old record for total offense and completions in one season with his performance against Tennessee.

end zone. Perry King missed the point-after kick.

When the Rebs got the ball again, Bob Knight fielded the Vols' punt and raced 49 yards to the Vol 16. Manning ran for 11 yards around left end and then passed to Riley Myers for the touchdown which put Ole Miss ahead, 19-0. Morris Felts swept outside for the two-point conversion which increased the Rebs' lead to 21-0.

Cloyce Hinton added a 42-yard field goal before halftime to bump the score to 24-0.

The Rebs' Fred Brister recovered a Vol fumble at the Tennessee 33 at the beginning of the third quarter. Manning wasted no time in trying to find the Vol end zone. He passed to Jimbo Poole for 12 yards, then sent Reed up to the Vol 1 on four carries. Manning jumped over right guard for the touchdown. Poole's extra-point kick made it 31-0.

The Rebs' final score came on a one-yard dive over left guard by Bowen which capped a 9-play, 74-yard drive. Poole's kick boosted the score to 38-0.

Ole Miss 27   Arkansas 22

January 1, 1970 | New Orleans, La.

Big Plays by Manning, Cannon Defeat Porkers

Archie Manning and Glenn Cannon had the 82,500 in Tulane Stadium shouting with joy. This dynamic duo pulled out big play after big play to defeat Arkansas, 27-22, today in the Sugar Bowl.

Cannon ended the Porkers' winning hopes when he fell on a Chuck Dicus fumble at the Rebel 28. Dicus had just caught a pass from Bill Montgomery, turned upfield and was given a jolting hit. He then lost the handle on the ball.

Manning completed 21 of 35 attempts for 273 yards and one touchdown. He also ran for one touchdown. His performance earned him The Miller-Digby Trophy as the game's most valuable player.

"I don't think our players realized how great he was," explained Arkansas coach Frank Broyles.

Montgomery put up some impressive stats, too. He threw for 17 completions on 34 attempts for 338 yards and a pair of touchdowns. He also added 28 yards rushing.

Overall, the Porkers outgained Ole Miss, 527 to 427 yards.

Ole Miss	14	10	3	0 —	27
Arkansas	0	12	3	7 —	22

Cannon turned in a heady afternoon. He broke up three passes on one drive and stole a Porkers' pass in the end zone from John Rees that would have been a touchdown.

Ole Miss pulled away early with a 14-0 lead.

Bo Bowen blasted up the middle on a trap play for 69 yards and the opening touchdown to put the Rebs up, 6-0. Cloyce Hinton's kick made it 7-0.

The Rebs marched 80 yards on the next touchdown. Vernon Studdard was the hero on this drive with his 57-yard reception that he outfought Dennis Berner for. Manning ran the final 18 yards to paydirt. Perry King's extra-point kick gave the Rebels a 14-0 lead.

The Porkers got on the scoreboard with a 82-yard march in the second quarter. Bill Burnett romped in from the Reb 12 for the touchdown.

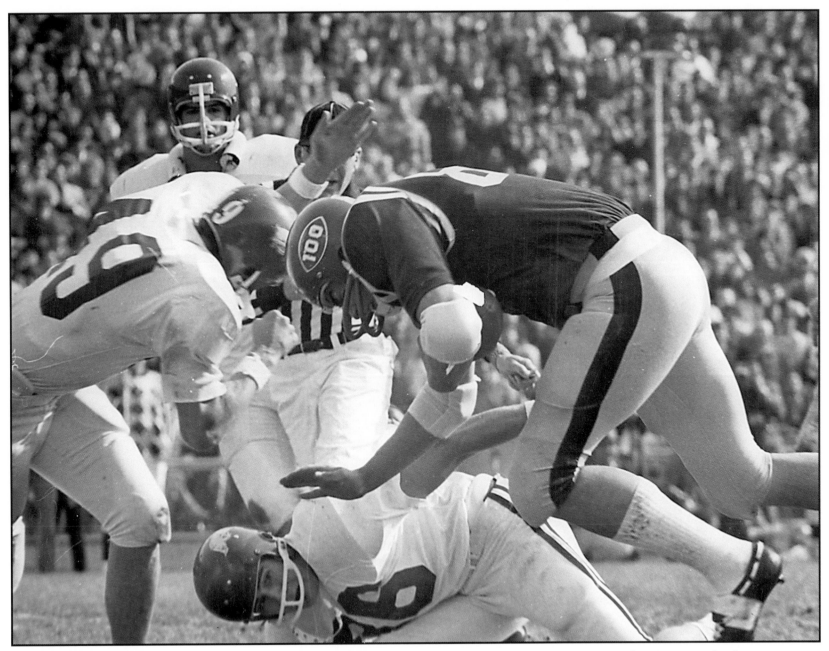

THE VAUGHT ERA

Rebel end Vernon Studdard (81) scored on a 30-yard pass from Archie Manning before halftime to give Ole Miss a 24-6 lead.

Bill Burnett (33), the Arkansas halfback, races 12 yards for a touchdown in the second quarter.

Top: Rebel halfback Randy Reed gets piled up by the Razorback defense led by Cliff Powell (64) and Mike Boschetti (59).

THE VAUGHT ERA

Bottom: Archie Manning passed for 273 yards and ran and passed for two touchdowns. He was named the Sugar Bowl's MVP.

Bill McClard's extra-point kick was wide and left the score at 14-6.

Hinton's record 52-yard field goal boosted the Rebs lead to 17-6.

Later, Manning's 30-yard pass to Studdard put the Rebels in command at 24-6.

Montgomery and Dicus then teamed up on a 47-yard touchdown pass before halftime that pulled the Porkers closer at 24-12.

In the third quarter, both teams traded field goals. Hinton booted a 36-yarder and Arkansas' McClard connected on a 35-yarder to increase the score to 27-15.

Montgomery's 6-yard touchdown pass to Bruce Maxwell got Arkansas back in the game, with the Rebs' lead reduced to 27-12.

But Cannon closed the door on the Porkers' hopes.

97

Ole Miss 48   Alabama 23

October 3, 1970 | Jackson, Miss.

Rebel Defense Outscores Tide in Epic Rematch

THE VAUGHT ERA

No. 7 Ole Miss paid back Bear Bryant's Crimson Tide for last year's 33-32 defeat tonight with a 48-23 whipping in front of a soldout crowd of 46,812 at Mississippi Memorial Stadium and a national television audience.

The Rebels are now 3-0 with prospects for a special season ahead.

Defense made the difference in this fierce rivalry.

The Rebels scored four touchdowns via the defense; one on a 100-yard kickoff return by wingback Vernon Studdard; another on a 9-play, 68-yard drive by Archie Manning; and one on a busted Alabama onside kick.

"We got some breaks early," Ole Miss coach John Vaught said, " then I thought 'Bama was coming back and we got some more breaks. The breaks let us get ahead and when you do you can take some chances."

"But football is a game of breaks," Vaught added.

The Rebels have now won two out of their last three meetings with Alabama. The Tide, however, leads the overall series, 22-4-2.

Ole Miss	14	12	0	22 —	48
Alabama	0	9	8	6 —	23

The Rebels got their first break when Bill VanDevender, the Rebs' monsterman, intercepted a Neb Hayden pass at the Alabama 29 and returned it to the 20. It took Manning and the Rebs five plays to reach the Tide end zone. Randy Reed scored on a 7-yard pass to put the Rebs up, 7-0.

On Ole Miss' next possession, Manning drove the Rebs 47 yards in 7 plays, with Manning diving over from the Tide 1 for the touchdown.

Alabama narrowed the score to 14-3 in the second quarter when Richard Ciemny booted a 36-yard field.

Studdard then struck with his 100-yard kickoff return for a touchdown to increase the Rebs' lead to 21-3. It was the 13th 100-yard kickoff return in SEC football history.

Manning worked his magic again when he cashed in on a touchdown after Fred Brister intercepted a Hayden pass and returned it to the Tide 14. Manning's touchdown pass to Reed bumped the Rebs to 26-3.

Alabama countered with a 15-yard touchdown strike from Hayden to Jerry Cash with 2:20 left in the second quarter.

Hayden added to that total in the third quarter on a 10-yard TD pass to Johnny Musso that tightened the score to 26-17.

Ole Miss got its biggest break when Alabama punter Frank Mann fumbled a deep snap at the Tide 26. Manning drove the Rebs in for the score in five plays, with Studdard snagging the 8-yard touchdown pass. Jimbo Poole added two points on a pass from Manning to give Ole Miss a 34-17 lead.

The Rebels added two more touchdowns on a 14-yard run by Manning and a 1-yard dive by Bob Knight to increase the tally to 48-17.

Alabama scored on a 19-yard pass from Hayden to Steve Doran which wrapped up the scoring at 48-23.

Far Left: Neb Hayden (11), who replaced Scott Hunter at quarterback, spent most of the evening eluding the Rebs' harrassing defense.

THE
VAUGHT
ERA

Left: Archie Manning (18) finished with 203 yards passing. He also rushed for two touchdowns and passed for three more.

101

THE
VAUGHT
ERA

ARCHIE:

GREATER THAN THE LEGEND

By Francis J. Fitzgerald

In the late 1960's and 1970 he rose from the status of a starting college quarterback to that of a Southern icon. They wrote a best-selling song about him — and it was carried on radio stations all over the South, fans wore buttons in support of him and displayed bumperstickers on their cars touting his wondrous feats, kids on every block wore his No. 18 jersey, motel marquees boasted that he had once slept there, and he graced the front covers of *Sports Illustrated* and *The Sporting News* and the entire front page of the largest Sunday newspaper in his home state after an unforgettable win against LSU.

He would win the Walter Camp Award as the most outstanding college football player in the country in 1969 and finished fourth in the voting for the Heisman Trophy in 1969 and third in 1970. And he married his school's homecoming queen.

He was a greater player than Joe Namath, Babe Parilli, Charlie Conerly, Steve Spurrier or Pat Sullivan. Better than any southern quarterback ever before or to follow him.

During this memorable time, he was better known throughout the South than grits or mason jars.

Elisha Archibald Manning III was all of this — and more.

The legend began in the small Delta town of Drew, Miss. Population 2,143. He was born on May 19, 1949, and grew up in a house across the street from Drew High School. He was given a football helmet by the local coach when he was 18 months old. And his older sister, Pam, recalls that he often slept with a football cradled in his arms. As a young boy he often stood on the corner outside the family home, watching the Drew High football team practice on the school grounds across the street.

Football was in his future, but in those boyhood years it seemed a long way off.

Baseball was a big part of his youth. Archie was taught by one of his uncles to bat left-handed and he earned the starting assignment at second base on the high school varsity when he was in seventh grade. Once in high school he became a phenom on the basketball team, played shortstop on the baseball team and quarterback on the football team.

When he first played for the Drew High baseball squad, Archie weighed only 100 pounds. The team didn't have regular baseball uniforms, so they wore old football jerseys.

"I bunted a lot and walked mostly, but I still hit .300," he later recalled.

The red-headed, freckled-face kid grew to be a lanky, 160 pounds and stood 6-foot-two, but he was embarrassed to go swimming without a T-shirt.

During the school week he got perfect grades and on Sunday he went to the First Baptist Church. When he left for college, he had gone 13 years without missing Sunday School.

There was, however, a flaw. As a youngster, the boy was always too busy to eat. This caused him to have the frail frame and several injuries in football. He broke his ankle in the eighth grade, his right arm in the 10th grade and his left arm in the 11th grade. Prior to his senior football season, he had played in only 12 games, winning just one.

IN THE FALL OF 1966, Archie led the Eagles to a 5-5 record, including an 18-14 upset over archrival Cleveland in his final game. He

THE VAUGHT ERA

Archie led Ole Miss to a 22-10 record in 1968-70.

During his varsity career at Ole Miss, Archie passed for 4,753 yards and 31 touchdowns.

received football scholarship offers from Ole Miss, Mississippi State and Tulane. Averaging nearly 30 points per game in basketball, he was widely recruited by college teams that season. As a shortstop who was blessed with a strong arm and could hit with power, he was drafted by the Atlanta Braves.

Archie would sign to play football for Ole Miss prior to Christmas 1966 in between the semi-finals and finals at the Coahoma County Invitational Basketball Tournament. Roy Stinnett, a Rebel graduate assistant, who was officiating the tourney, was assigned by Ole Miss coach John Vaught to get Archie's signature on the grant-in-aid.

It was the only school he ever wanted to play for.

In the Mississippi High

THE VAUGHT ERA

Archie finished fourth in the Heisman Trophy balloting in 1969 and third in 1970.

105

The College Football Hall of Fame inducted Archie into its Class of 1989.

freshmen squads.

In the fall of 1968, Archie led Ole Miss to a 7-3-1 record while passing for 1,510 yards on 127 completions in 263 attempts and eight TD's. He also rushed for 209 yards and five touchdowns.

His first touchdown pass was to tailback Steve Hindman which went for 13 yards in his debut against Memphis State. He later connected with Hindman, on a six-yard TD pass and ran for two yards for a touchdown. This auspicious start earned him The Associated Press' "Player of the Week" honor.

After a 3-0 start, with wins over Memphis State (21-7), Kentucky (34-14) and Alabama (10-8), Manning & Co. would lose to Georgia, 21-7.

Billy Kinard, an assistant on Vince Dooley's staff at Georgia and later the coach of the Rebel's after Manning departed, had scouted the Ole Miss-Alabama game. He would report to Dooley: "They haven't had a quarterback like this boy in a while. He's good on the sprintouts and they like to run."

Injuries in the game to key Reb defenders Glenn Cannon and Frank Trapp as well as to Manning, who sprained the thumb on his throwing hand, slowed down Ole Miss, which lost 21-7.

Three weeks later, Archie brought Ole Miss back from a 17-3 deficit to a 27-24 victory in Tiger Stadium. In this rally, he threw for 24 com-

School All-Star Game that summer, he came off the bench and led the North All-Stars, who were coached by Meridian High's Bob Tyler, to a 57-33 victory by passing for four touchdowns and running for one.

Vaught called him, "the most outstanding prospect of all of the quarterbacks I've ever coached."

As a freshman on the Baby Rebs, he completed 30 of 55 passes for 497 yards, seven touchdowns, no interceptions and ran for 24 yards and 1 TD and defeated the Alabama, LSU, Vandy and Mississippi State

pletions in 40 attempts for 345 yards and a pair of touchdowns. After the game, he was named The Associated Press' National Back of the Week.

The low point of the season came two weeks later against Tennessee in Knoxville. Archie threw six interceptions and Ole Miss lost, 31-0.

The Vols' all-American linebacker, Steve Kiner, noted after the game, "He looks where he's throwing."

Archie and the Rebs would bounce back with a 34-17 win over Virginia Tech in the Liberty Bowl.

ONE WEEK PRIOR to the beginning of fall practice for the 1968 season, Archie's father died. It would make a major impact in his life.

"He grew up in two minutes," his sister Pam explained. "Any decision made in our household after that, Archie was the one to make it."

This new maturity allowed Archie to take the Rebels to greater glory. He had also grown up in other ways. At 6 3½ and 205 pounds, he could run the 100-yard dash in 10.2 seconds and was ready to run into the middle of an opposing defense.

But Ole Miss was having a tough time getting out of the gate. The Rebels were picked as the Southeastern Conference's preseason favorite,

Archie was selected as an all-American in 1969.

along with Georgia, and were rated No. 9 in The Associated Press' preseason poll.

After blasting Memphis State, 28-3, the heavily-favored Rebs lost to Kentucky, 10-9.

A week later, on a hot, humid night in Birmingham on national television, Archie and Alabama quarterback Scott Hunter dueled in the greatest game ever played in SEC football history.

Ole Miss would lose, 33-32, but Archie's performance struck a nerve with those who were watching the game on tv. He accounted for five Rebel touchdowns — passing for three touchdowns and running for two more, while racking up 540 yards in total offense. Hunter passed for 300 yards with 22 completions on 29 attempts.

The next week against Georgia, after hurting his neck late in the first half, Archie returned in the third quarter accompanied by a wild ovation. He rallied the Rebs from a 17-13 deficit to a 25-17 victory.

Following the game, Vaught noted, "The team has tremendous confidence in him. They've seen him do so many things under adverse conditions to pull out a game."

Against No. 8-ranked LSU, who was considered the strongest defensive team in the SEC, Archie accounted for all of the Rebs' points —

107

running for three touchdowns, passing for another and scored again on a two-point conversion run in a 26-23 win. Archie threw for 22 completions on 36 attempts for 210 yards.

After the contest, Frank J. Polozola, a Baton Rouge attorney filed a lawsuit in federal court seeking an injunction to prevent Archie from "further harassment" of the LSU team.

In the Rebs' third game in Jackson that season, Archie & Co. repaid Tennessee for their 31-0 loss the previous season. The Vols were 8-0 and ranked No. 3 in the country going into the game.

Kiner, the Vols' all-American linebacker, had poked fun at the Rebels before the game, calling them "mules."

Archie and the Reb defense responded by shutting out the Vols, 38-0. Archie completed 9 of 18 passes for 159 yards and one touchdown.

The win earned the Rebs a Sugar Bowl berth against Arkansas, who had only lost to No. 1-ranked Texas.

Ole Miss would win on New Year's Day, 27-22. Archie finished the afternoon with 21 completions in 35 attempts for 273 yards, plus 39 yards on the ground, and had one passing and one running touchdown. He also was voted the winner of The Miller-Digby Trophy as the game's most valuable player.

With the best-selling "The Ballad of Archie Who" echoing in their ears, Ole Miss fans were waiting in anticipation of a magical autumn in 1970.

THE 1970 REBELS' SEASON was billed in neon lights as "the Season." It was to be a season to shine over all others.

But the hatchet that has axed many great dreams fell.

It began in the second game of the season when Archie pulled a groin muscle in the Rebs' 20-17 win over Kentucky.

The next two weeks, although limited to standing in the pocket and rifling the pin-point passes, Archie passed the Rebs past Alabama, 48-23, on national tv, and Georgia, 31-21, in a duel between the edges.

Against Southern Mississippi, Archie struck for 341 yards on 30 of 56 passes, but the Golden Eagles were perfect in a 30-14 win.

The week of the Vanderbilt game, Vaught suffered a heart attack, but Archie kept the Rebels focused and defeated the Commodores, 26-16.

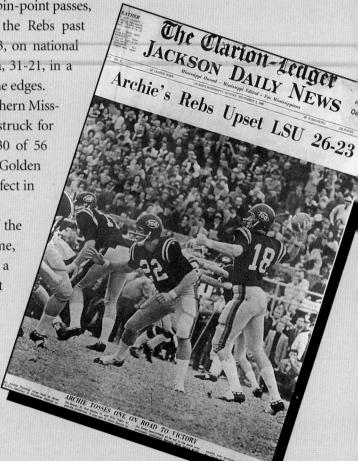

The Clarion-Ledger
JACKSON DAILY NEWS
Archie's Rebs Upset LSU 26-23

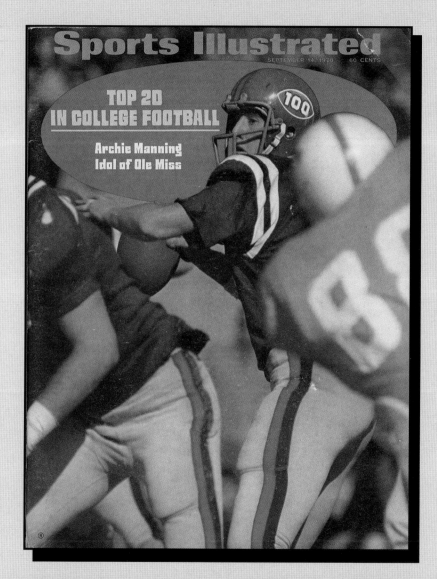

After a banner season in 1969, Archie was selected to appear on the front cover of *Sports Illustrated*'s 1970 pre-season college football issue.

The Manning Record

	RUSHING			PASSING			
	Yards	Carries	TD	Yards	Comp.	Att.	TD
1968	208	110	5	1,510	127	263	8
1969	502	124	14	1,762	154	265	9
1970	114	80	6	1,481	121	233	14
TOTAL	824	314	25	4,753	402	761	31

THE VAUGHT ERA

Two weeks later, Archie broke his left arm in the third quarter in a 24-13 win over Houston. At the end of the season, Archie returned to the lineup against LSU. With his left arm protected by a elbow-length plastic cast and slowed by a month of watching from the sideline, LSU enacted a dose of revenge for the Rebels' previous two wins in 1968 and 1969 by routing Ole Miss, 61-17.

A few weeks later, in the Gator Bowl against Auburn, Archie tried to go out a winner. And though he scampered for 95 yards on 11 carries and passed for 180 yards and one touchdown on 19 completions in 28 attempts, the Tigers managed to win, 35-28.

The following spring, Archie was the second player drafted in the 1971 National Football League draft. He would eventually play for 14 seasons in the NFL with the New Orleans Saints, the Minnesota Vikings and the Houston Oilers.

109

Ole Miss 41   Southern Miss 0

THE VAUGHT ERA

Vaught Returns and Leads Ole Miss to Glory

John Vaught returned as coach of the Ole Miss Rebels today and immediately corrected the team's football fortunes with a 41-0 whipping of cross-state rival Southern Mississippi.

A crowd of 31,500 in Hemingway Stadium sang "Happy Days Are Here Again" when it was all over.

A banner unfurled by the Ole Miss cheerleaders which proclaimed, "Ole Miss is Back," accurately described the feeling that rested in the hearts of all Rebel fans.

The victory evened the Rebels' record at 2 wins and 2 losses.

The win this afternoon ended a week of turmoil at the Oxford campus which began with the firings of Frank (Bruiser) Kinard as the school's athletic director and his brother, Billy, as the football coach.

Vaught, who had retired after the 1970 season to a life of playing golf and tending to his farm outside of town, was summoned by Dr. Porter Fortune, the school's chancellor, to take over for the remainder of the season.

Vaught's shuffled staff opened the game with a deep pass from quar-

Southern Miss.	0	0	0	0 —	0
Ole Miss	0	13	7	21 —	41

terback Kenny Lyons to wide receiver Rick Kimbrough that fell just beyond his reach. The play appeared to catch the Eagles off guard.

And though the Rebels appeared to look confused in the first quarter with a pair of fumbles and some late arrivals from the bench, that first play was an example of the wide-open attack that the Rebels would employ.

"We wanted to give 'em something to think about," Vaught later explained.

One of the fumbles occurred at the Reb 1 after Lyons was sacked while attempting to pass at the Reb 18.

Hemingway Stadium got amazingly quiet when Eagle fullback Wilson Plunkett swept around right end toward the Reb goal line. The silence was shattered when Billy May, a Reb defensive tackle, hit

Ole Miss chancellor, Dr. Porter Fortune, announces to the press that John Vaught will return from retirement to lead Ole Miss for the remainder of the 1973 season.

THE VAUGHT ERA

With less than a minute left in the first half, Lavinghouze booted another field goal which increased the Rebs' lead to 13-0.

Ole Miss opened the second half with a fireworks display.

Rebel fullback Gene Allen raced 78 yards from the Reb 17 to the Southern Miss 5 on their first possession. James Reed rammed off tackle on two plays to reach the Eagles' end zone.

Southern Miss tried to mount a brief comeback when Bower drove the Eagles to the Reb 12, but defensive end Gary Turner slammed him on a passing attempt, causing a fumble which Ole Miss recovered.

Dan Murff, who switched from defensive back to the offensive backfield when Vaught took over, ran for two touchdowns on short runs of two and three yards.

Backup quarterback Stan Bounds, a sophomore, then threw a 22-yard touchdown pass to split end Danny Stallings.

Turner and Williams made the difference all afternoon as they harassed Bower everytime he went back to pass.

Plunkett at the Reb 2 and knocked the ball loose. The Rebs' Robert Arnold recovered the ball at the Reb 7.

Ole Miss soon found its groove.

After Ben Williams pounded Southern quarterback Jeff Bower, who fumbled the ball, the Rebels took over at the Eagle 44. Lyons marched the Rebs to the Eagle end zone in 10 plays. Steve Lavinghouze booted the extra-point kick to give Ole Miss a 7-0 lead with 9:11 left in the second quarter.

Lavinghouze added a 32-yard field goal to boost the score to 10-0.

"They were a good football team today," Golden Eagles coach P.W. (Bear) Underwood, explained in the USM dressing room after the game. "We knew we had to do something early to bring them down from the clouds. If we could have gotten on the scoreboard first when we had a chance, it might have established the momentum and changed the game."

But in the end it would not have mattered because this was John Vaught and Ole Miss' day.

A LEGEND

A LEGEND
OLE MISS
ALMOST MISSED

By Francis J. Fitzgerald

THE VAUGHT ERA

At age 90, he spends his days on the golf course and relaxing on his farm outside Oxford, Miss. But once, he was one of the greatest coaches in the history of college football.

From 1947 to 1970 and briefly in 1973 John Howard Vaught ruled the Ole Miss sidelines with a vengeance. During 25 seasons at the helm of the Rebel juggernaut he posted a record of 190 wins, 61 losses and 12 ties, won six Southeastern Conference titles and three national championships and played in 18 bowl games.

However, except for a strange twist of fate Vaught and Ole Miss almost never got together.

Vaught was born in the North Texas town of Olney, grew up in Fort Worth and played fullback there for Polytechnic High, where he earned All-City honors. In the classroom he was valedictorian of his class. At Texas Christian University, he was a three-year starter at left guard and captained the Horned Frogs team as a senior in 1932 as well as being named to the All-Southwest Conference and all-America teams.

The Horned Frogs, under Francis Schmidt's tutelage, were becoming a dominant powerhouse in the Southwest Conference. Following the

1932 season, Vaught and five of the seven TCU linemen earned All-Southwest Conference. But the toughest of the bunch was Vaught, who at 195 lbs. was always the first Horned Frog downfield to make a bone-bruising tackle.

After graduation, he coached for two seasons at Fort Worth's North Side High but the wages were meager during the Depression, so he left coaching and went crosstown to join Graybar Electric.

In the spring of 1936, Ray (Bear) Wolf, who had coached the TCU

Vaught at practice with quarterbacks Kenny Lyons (left) and Norris Weese at practice during the 1973 season.

line when Vaught played there, telephoned him to ask him to join his staff at North Carolina. He would coach with Wolf for six seasons. When World War II arrived, Vaught enlisted and spent the next four years coaching in the Navy Pre-Flight program.

He arrived in Oxford in 1946 as an assistant to Harold (Red) Drew. His assignment would be coaching the Rebel line. That Fall, Ole Miss managed to win only 2 games and lost seven.

A few months later, just before the 1947 spring practice was to begin, Drew was offered the opportunity to replace the retiring coaching legend, Frank Thomas, at Alabama and he wanted to take Vaught with him.

Upon hearing this, Tad Smith, then the athletic director at Ole Miss, called Vaught into his office intent on offering him the Rebels' head coaching job.

He asked, "John, are you ambitious?"

"I certainly am," Vaught replied.

Ambitious perhaps, but not convinced of Ole Miss' commitment to winning at the time.

"I wanted to be the head coach,"

Former Tulane all-American tailback Monk Simmons awards John Vaught the 1960 Sugar Bowl Trophy after their win over LSU.

Vaught would later explain. "But I was concerned about what kind of chances we had for success at Ole Miss. I was also concerned about getting our share of the Mississippi boys. During this time most of the state's top high school players were going to Mississippi State."

A few days later, Smith had Vaught in his office, trying once more to convince him to take the Ole Miss job. At that time, the remainder of Drew's staff were packed in two cars outside Smith's office, waiting impatiently to take them to Tuscaloosa.

"They kept yelling and honking, 'Come on. Johnny,' " Smith recalled. "Finally, Vaught told them, 'I'm not going.'

"I knew if anyone could lead Ole Miss out of the wilderness, John Vaught was the one to do it," Smith added.

Before Vaught took the Ole Miss job, 26 coaches had tried to turn the Rebels into winners. All had moved on with varying degrees of success — or the lack of it.

Three notable coaches among this group all found failure there: Homer Hazel, an all-American back at Rutgers in the great days of

Vaught's 1960 National Championship team posted a record of 10-0-1 and defeated Rice, 14-6, in the 1960 Sugar Bowl.

THE VAUGHT ERA

Big East football; Ed Walker, a star pupil of Pop Warner; and Harry Mehre, a Knute Rockne protege, who came to Ole Miss after ten seasons at the University of Georgia.

Hazel lasted five seasons, Walker eight and Mehre seven. Their combined record was 98 wins, 85 losses and 12 ties.

Before Vaught, the Rebels had never won more than three league games in a season.

Yet in his first season, Vaught at age 37, old enough to respect the fundamentals and yet young enough to gamble, managed to win nine games, lost two and captured the school's first SEC title.

The team he inherited was led by Charlie Conerly, a multi-talented tailback, and Barney Poole, a 23-year-old junior end who had played his sophomore year in Oxford in 1942, then at North Carolina as a marine trainee in 1943, and on West Point's great teams of 1944-45-46. Service

115

football didn't count against eligibility in this era, so Poole still had two more years left to play for the Rebels.

Vaught wasted no time in putting together a hybrid offense to utilize the special abilities of this unique duo.

Conerly's greatest show came during a 43-13 conquest of Tennessee in Memphis. It was a memorable afternoon on two counts: it was the first time Ole Miss had beaten Tennessee in twenty tries; it also was the worst defeat ever inflicted on Tennessee coach Robert Neyland.

Conerly completed 19 of 34 passes for 246 yards and four touchdowns and ran twelve times for 45 yards while Ole Miss rolled up 426 yards of offense.

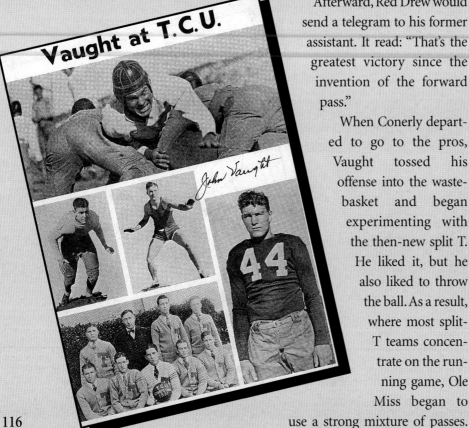

Vaught at T.C.U.

John Vaught

Afterward, Red Drew would send a telegram to his former assistant. It read: "That's the greatest victory since the invention of the forward pass."

When Conerly departed to go to the pros, Vaught tossed his offense into the wastebasket and began experimenting with the then-new split T. He liked it, but he also liked to throw the ball. As a result, where most split-T teams concentrate on the running game, Ole Miss began to use a strong mixture of passes.

Especially the sprintout.

"We've got a pass off almost every run play and a run off almost every pass play," Vaught once told a visiting sportswriter.

The Rebels had a few lean seasons after Conerly's departure, but things began to click in 1951 — and for two decades Ole Miss was one of the SEC's crown jewels.

Beginning in 1952, the Rebels would play on New Year's Day in either the Sugar Bowl or the Cotton Bowl 10 times over the next 18 seasons.

They would win SEC titles in 1954, 1955, 1960, 1962 and 1963. And were ranked No. 1 in the nation in 1959, 1960 and 1962 in certain polls. And for four seasons — 1959 to 1962 — his Rebels owned the college football world.

And he could coach magnificent passers. Immortals such as Charley Conerly, Eagle Day, Ray Brown, Bobby Franklin, Jake Gibbs, Billy Brewer, Glynn Griffing and Archie Manning.

His most shining moment may have been the Rebels' 21-0 revenge win over LSU in the 1960 Sugar Bowl after a disappointing 7-3 loss to the Tigers on Halloween Night 1959 when eventual Heisman winner Billy Cannon ran 89 yards for a game-winning touchdown and a big slice of immortality.

By the mid-1960's Paul (Bear) Bryant and Alabama had begun to steal all of the thunder in the SEC.

But in the late 1960's and 1970, with Archie Manning as his quarterback, Vaught had one more run in the spotlight.

For three seasons, from 1968 to 1970, Vaught and Bryant's teams tangled in three unforgettable games. Ole Miss won, 10-8, in Jackson in 1968. A year later, Manning and Alabama quarterback Scott Hunter battled in the greatest passing duel in SEC history, with Alabama managing to pull out a 33-32 win. In Jackson in 1970, Manning & Co. bounced back to win handily, 48-23.

Vaught would suffer a heart attack during the 1970 season and he retired after the Rebels played Auburn in the Gator Bowl.

But less than three seasons later, in late September 1973, Ole Miss

Vaught and his two great quarterbacks, Archie Manning (left) and Charlie Conerly (right).

THE VAUGHT ERA

The Vaught Record

	W	L	T
1947 (1)	9	2	0
1948	8	1	0
1949	4	5	1
1950	5	5	0
1951	6	3	1
1952	8	1	2
1953	7	2	1
1954 (1)	9	2	0
1955 (1)	10	1	0
1956	7	3	0
1957	9	1	1
1958	9	2	0
1959 (2)	10	1	0
1960 (1) (2)	10	0	1
1961	9	2	0
1962 (1) (2)	10	0	0
1963 (1)	7	1	2
1964	5	5	1
1965	7	4	0
1966	8	3	0
1967	6	4	1
1968	7	3	1
1969	8	3	0
1970	7	4	0
1973	4	4	0
TOTAL	190	61	12

(1) SEC Champions
(2) National Champions

asked him to lead them out of the darkness once again when the university's administration sacked Billy Kinard as the football coach and his brother, Bruiser Kinard, as the athletic director.

Vaught led the Rebels to a record of four wins and four losses in 1973, including back-to-back late-season wins over Tennessee, 28-18, and Mississippi State, 38-10.

After restoring once again the pride in the Rebels, he would retire for good.

117

THE DIFFICULT YEARS

"We won this game for a great kid, Chucky Mullins."

OLE MISS HEAD COACH BILLY BREWER

Ole Miss 10   Alabama 7

September 11, 1976 l Jackson, Miss.

Stunning Rebs Choke Alabama's SEC Win Streak

Hoppy Langley booted Ole Miss to a 10-7 shocking win over Alabama tonight in Mississippi Memorial Stadium in front of a crowd of 47,500. The loss stopped an Alabama 11-game win streak and a string of 20 consecutive SEC victories.

The Tide's last conference loss was in 1972 against Auburn.

Langley, a freshman placekicker, connected on a 34-yard field goal with 13:01 left in the fourth quarter to give the Rebels the 10-7 lead and then played outstanding defense against the powerhouse Alabama wishbone attack.

The victory is one of the greatest in school history and gives Ole Miss the lead in the SEC title hunt. The Rebels entered the contest as 14-point underdogs.

"This is one of the biggest I can remember," John Vaught, the Ole Miss athletic director, said from the press box at the end of the game." I can only remember one other game that ranks with this one, and that was the Maryland game."

Alabama	0	0	7	0 —	7
Ole Miss	7	0	0	3 —	10

That win came in 1952 when Ole Miss defeated Maryland in Oxford. The victory put Ole Miss in the national spotlight and allowed Vaught to build the Rebels into a prominent football power.

Rebel coach Ken Cooper explained his team's win after the game: "It was just an old-fashioned defensive football game with Ole Miss just managing to put enough points on the scoreboard to win. You can credit our defense with a super effort. And credit the entire team with a great effort, too.

"It took a lot of bounce to come back from that loss to Memphis State. We wanted to show folks we could come back because I think we've got that kind of team. I wouldn't say it's a beautiful win, but it sure is mighty sweet."

Bryant, who had received 63 roses from his team prior to the game,

120

Rebel end Gary Turner (88) batted down a Jeff Rutledge (11) pass, which Ole Miss linebacker George Stuart intercepted and returned for an Ole Miss touchdown.

121

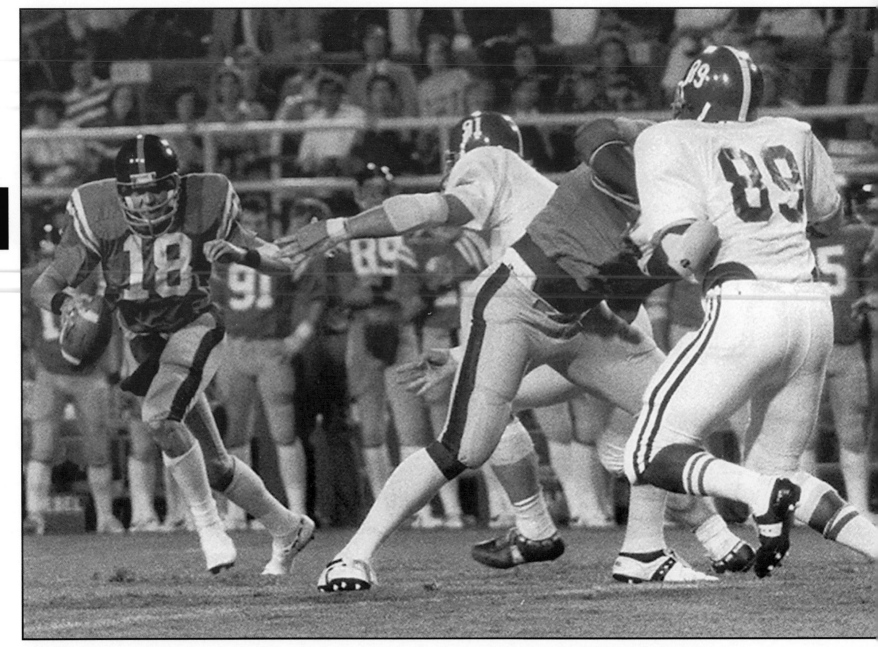

Tim Ellis (18), the Rebels' quarterback, rolls right to escape the hard rush of Alabama lineman Bob Baumhauer (91).

bragged on the Rebels following the game.

"I'd like to congratulate Coach Cooper and his staff for really having their team ready to play," Bryant said. "I thought they played a really hard game. They really came after us.

"Their defense controlled the line of scrimmage against us. We couldn't throw the football and we couldn't move it with any kind of consistence, and they forced us to make a lot of mistakes. Their kicking game also hurt us. They had some real fine ones (punts) in the clutch, and I guess I should have started my talk with that — the kicking game, because that's what won for them."

Alabama entered the game ranked No. 6 in the country.

The game turned when Ole Miss linebacker George Stuart intercepted a deflected pass from Tide quarterback Jeff Rutledge at the Alabama 24. Stuart caught the ball after it had been batted

George Stuart runs past Tide end Ozzie Newsome (82) en route to his 24-yard interception return for a touchdown with 3:54 left in the first quarter.

in the air by Reb defensive end Gary Turner. Stuart sprinted into the Alabama end zone for the touchdown with 3:54 left in the first quarter. Langley added the point-after kick.

Alabama got on the scoreboard with 7:22 left in the third quarter

when Calvin Culliver burst over from the Reb 3 for the touchdown.

The Tide almost scored after Tide cornerback Mike Tucker picked up a Rebel fumble at their 47 and ran with it to the Reb 25. Alabama's drive was stopped by a fumble that was recovered by Turner.

THE DIFFICULT YEARS

Ole Miss 20   Notre Dame 13

September 17, 1977 | Jackson, Miss.

Ole Miss Shocks No. 3-Ranked Fighting Irish

Notre Dame came to the Old South today and was administered an old-fashioned, "behind-the-toolshed" 20-13 whipping by Ken Cooper's Rebels at Mississippi Memorial Stadium in front of an overflow crowd of 48,200.

John Vaught, who will be retiring soon as Ole Miss' athletic director, called it "one of the great Ole Miss victories of all-time."

Playing in a sticky 85-degree heat, the Rebs called on third-string quarterback Tim Ellis to lead his team to a go-ahead touchdown with 3:28 remaining in the game on a 10-yard pass to fullback James Storey.

Storey's scoring run gave the Rebs a 17-13 lead.

Hoppy Langley added to this lead with a 27-yard field goal less than two minutes later after Brian Moreland intercepted an Irish pass.

Moreland also intercepted the pass that sealed the Irish's fate with 17 seconds left in the game.

Most of the Rebel fans hung around the stadium after the game, savoring the victory they had just seen.

Notre Dame	0	7	0	6 —	13
Ole Miss	3	7	0	10 —	20

Vaught called it a milepost win for the Rebels and Cooper.

"A game like this …" Vaught explained, "well, it's the kind of thing that can put this team in the frame of mind to go ahead and develop the program. This is a football team, and now I imagine they know it themselves."

The Irish didn't look like the No. 3-ranked team in the country.

Ole Miss owned the game and the final stats. The Rebs had 157 yards rushing to Notre Dame's 147, passed for 194 yards to the Irish's 127 and finished with 351 total yards to Notre Dame's 274.

George Plasketes and Charlie Cage led an Ole Miss defense that kept the Irish offense busy.

Plasketes had 15 tackles and Cage 14.

Moreland, a second-team linebacker, got in the game when starter

Ken Coleman injured an ankle. Moreland wasted no time making his presence known.

Ellis entered the game after Notre Dame kicker Dave Reeve booted an 8-yard field goal that put the Irish ahead, 13-10. The 3-pointer capped an 80-yard drive.

Ellis took over at the Ole Miss 20. He tossed a 10-yard pass to Curtis Weathers, then flinged a 47-yarder to L.Q. Smith, a substitute tight end from Oxford, Miss., who brought the crowd to its feet with his stirring run to the Irish 23.

Storey rambled to the Irish 10, then Ellis tossed a 10-yard to Storey for the go-ahead touchdown.

The Rebels scored first this afternoon with a 29-yard field goal by Langley which gave Ole Miss a 3-0 lead.

Jerome Heavens put the Irish ahead with a 2-yard run just before halftime.

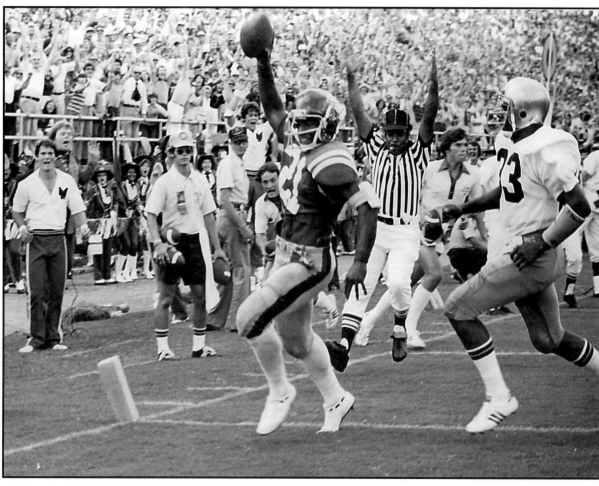

James Storey's fourth-quarter 10-yard touchdown reception sealed the Rebs' 20-13 upset win over Notre Dame at Mississippi Memorial Stadium.

THE DIFFICULT YEARS

Ole Miss managed to drive 76 yards before the halftime buzzer to retake the lead at 10-7. A Bobby Garner pass to Roy Coleman traveled 52 yards. Garner then passed to Storey for a 9-yard TD pass.

Notre Dame tied the score at 10-10 when Reeve kicked a 44-yard field goal.

A Reb fumble early in the fourth quarter set the Irish up for their scoring drive. Reeve's 26-yard field goal broke the tie, putting the Irish ahead, 13-10.

Ellis then went to work and redeemed an Ole Miss squad that had been embarrassed by Alabama, 34-14, a week earlier.

"We just keep coming back," Cooper explained. "We always seemed somehow to come up with the big play."

125

Ole Miss 21   Mississippi State 17

November 21, 1981 | Jackson, Miss.

Fourcade Sparkles in Rebs' Upset Win Over State

THE DIFFICULT YEARS

The John Fourcade era at Ole Miss ended with as much drama as the past four years of his career.

Playing in his final game as a Rebel, the Gretna, La., senior drove his team on a 60-yard scoring march in the last 30 seconds of the fourth quarter that gave Ole Miss a 21-17 win over cross-state rival Mississippi State at Mississippi Memorial Stadium this afternoon.

The loss put a dent in Mississippi State's celebration plans after accepting a bid to play in the Dec. 31 Hall of Fame Bowl in Birmingham.

But most of the crowd of 61,153 cheered the Rebels' come-from-behind victory.

The Rebs winning score came on a one-yard run by Fourcade with just two seconds left. It was set up by a 24-yard pass interference penalty against Mississippi State in the end zone.

The final four minutes were perhaps the wildest ending ever in the 78-game history of the series.

Ole Miss	7	0	0	14 —	21
Mississippi State	0	14	0	3 —	17

With State leading, 14-7, midway through the fourth quarter, the Rebs drove 76 yards to tie the score at 14-14. Fourcade ran the final 10 yards for the touchdown with 3:37 left in the game.

Wasting no time, the Bulldogs drove 72 yards to the Ole Miss 10. With only 35 seconds left, Dana Moore booted a 27-yard field goal to put State in the lead, 17-14..

With 30 seconds remaining, Fourcade went to work. Beginning at the Reb 22, he first fired a pass to Michael Harmon at the Reb 41. He then found Harmon open again at the State 43.

Then, with the ball at the State 25 and 13 seconds left, came the interference play that moved the ball to the State 1 and Fourcade's game-winning run.

Bulldogs fans, however, contested the penalty call. Harmon, the

THE
DIFFICULT
YEARS

John Fourcade (1) races one yard for the game-winning TD against Mississippi State in the game's final seconds.

intended receiver, and State defender Kenneth Johnson both went up in the air for the ball and fought for it at the State 1.

After the play, State fans thought Johnson had stopped a touchdown. But the official, Dick Pace of Maitland, Fla., saw it differently and awarded the Rebs the ball at the Bulldogs' 1. One play later, Fourcade then danced into history.

Ole Miss scored first in the contest on a 74-yard drive in five plays. Fourcade's 39-yard touchdown pass to Andre Thomas with 13:08 put the Rebs ahead, 7-0.

In the second quarter, State drove 51 yards in 12 plays for the Bulldogs' first score. Fullback Donald Ray King dove over the final yard for the touchdown. Bob Morgan's extra-point kick tied it up at 7-7 with 8:51 left in the half.

State scored again after Johnie Cooks knocked the ball loose from Reb halfback Malvin Gipson at the Reb 29. Defensive end Mike McEnany made the recovery for State.

The Bulldogs scored in five

Bulldog all-American linebacker Johnie Cooks (99) had to keep up with John Fourcade all afternoon.

plays, with Danny Knight sweeping around left end for the last five yards for the touchdown. Morgan's kick increased State's lead to 14-7 at halftime.

State had two scoring opportunities fizzle out in the third quarter on drives that reached the Reb 17 and the Reb 27.

Fourcade's final game was one of his finest ever in a Rebel jersey. He completed 21 of 29 attempts for 240 yards and a touchdown and ran for two more.

Ole Miss now leads the series with State, 44-28-6.

Ole Miss coach Steve Sloan enjoys being carried off the field by his players. Sloan defeated the Bulldogs on three of 5 meetings.

129

Ole Miss 21   Louisiana State 19

November 1, 1986 | Baton Rouge, La.

Rebels End Drought Against No. 12 LSU Tigers

Ole Miss proved possible the impossible today when they defeated No. 12 LSU, 21-19, in Tiger Stadium in front of a crowd of 77,778.

It was the Rebels' first win in Tiger Stadium since 1968 and fourth straight of the season.

LSU had the opportunity to win the game but a 30-yard field goal by Tiger place-kicker David Browndyke was wide left with only nine seconds left.

"What a way to win," Billy Brewer, the excited Rebels' coach shouted as he was carried off the field.

After the game, Brewer called it his biggest win as a coach.

Browndyke, a freshman from Dallas, Tex., who was playing in only his second college game, booted field goals of 40, 31, 52 and 21 yards before missing two in the final quarter that would have made the difference for the Tigers.

With only 59 seconds left and trailing, 21-19, Tiger quarterback Tommy Hodson completed four passes to receiver Wendell Davis and

Ole Miss	7	14	0	0	—	21
LSU	6	3	7	3	—	19

LSU traveled from their 34 to the Reb 13.

With only 14 seconds on the scoreboard clock, Browndyke jogged onto the field to kick the Tigers to victory. He kicked from the right hash mark — but the ball sailed left.

Browndyke had kicked seven straight field goals prior to missing a 52-yarder earlier in the fourth quarter.

"I wasn't too nervous, I just didn't kick it well," Browndyke explained.

Ole Miss is now 6-2-1 and 3-1 in the Southeastern Conference.

The Rebs led, 21-9, at halftime.

Early in the third quarter, LSU defensive end Roland Barbay stripped the ball from Reb quarterback Mark Young at the Ole Miss 27, with Tiger linebacker Oliver Lawrence making the recovery. Two plays later, Hodson passed to Davis, who was streaking down the sideline for a 29-

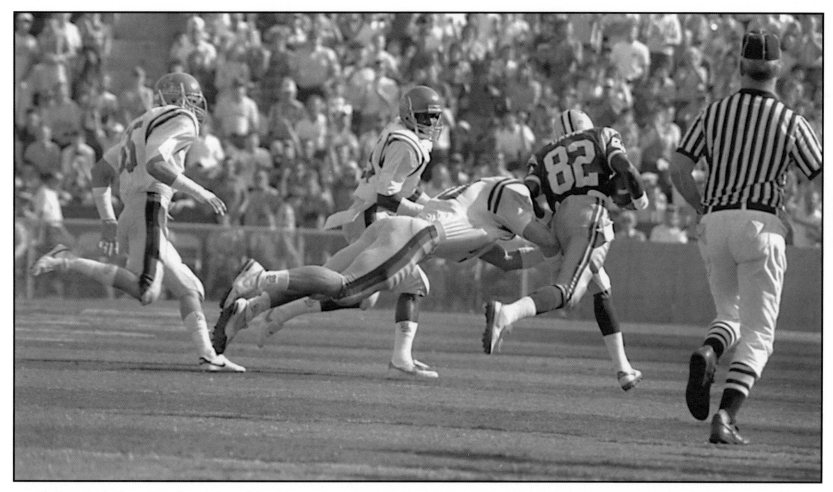

Wendell Davis (82) sprints down the sideline for a 29-yard TD in the third quarter, which reduced the Rebs' lead to 21-16.

THE DIFFICULT YEARS

yard touchdown. Browndyke's point-after kick narrowed the score to 21-16.

Davis would finish the game with 14 receptions for 208 yards.

Browndyke's field goal with 12:09 left in the final quarter reduced the Rebs' lead to 21-19. The field goal was his fourth of the game, tying a school record.

LSU got an early 6-0 lead on a pair of Browndyke field goals.

But the Rebels, who were playing in front of eight bowl scouts, came back.

Young drove his team on a 13-play, 75-yard march that was capped by J.R. Ambrose's 23-yard TD run. Bryan Owen added the point-after kick to give Ole Miss a 7-6 lead late in the first quarter.

Reb receiver Ricky Myers (25) cuts upfield after making a reception against the Tigers.

THE DIFFICULT YEARS

Fullback Tony Dentley (40) romped five yards for a second-quarter touchdown.

On their next possession, the Rebs marched 83 yards, with fullback Tony Dentley running the final five yards for a touchdown. The Rebs then lead, 14-6.

Browndyke's 52-yard field goal closed the gap to 14-9.

Young then scored before halftime on a 2-yard run to boost the Rebs' lead to 21-9. Young completed nine passes on the drive.

The Reb quarterback finished the game with 18 completions on 31 attempts for 171 yards. Hodson had 21 completions on 39 attempts for 251 yards. LSU, who fell to 5-2 and 3-1 in the SEC, led in total yardage, 399 to 316.

133

Ole Miss 22   Alabama 12

October 8, 1988 | Tuscaloosa, Ala.

Rebs Get First Win Over Tide in T-Town

THE DIFFICULT YEARS

S hawn Sykes, an unlikely Ole Miss hero who rushed for two touchdowns, led the Rebels' 22-12 upset of No. 12-ranked Alabama in Bryant-Denny Stadium. It was the Rebs' first win over Alabama in Tuscaloosa.

A crowd of 70,123 were on hand for an expected Homecoming victory and the dedication of the new Paul (Bear) Bryant Museum.

Sykes scored on runs of 53 and 12 yards to power the Rebs this afternoon, who entered the game as 18-point underdogs and 0-14 in previous trips to Tuscaloosa.

After the game, Ole Miss coach Billy Brewer and his players stayed out on the field to soak up the celebration mood.

Brewer, whose Rebs were coming off a 3-8 season in 1987, was especially proud of this win.

"We were coming off probation, we were gutted last year, we lost support and everybody was questioning everybody from the coaches to the guy who parked the cars," Brewer explained to the assembled press

Ole Miss	0	0	7	15 —	22
Alabama	0	0	12	0 —	12

in the Rebs' locker room.

"I felt like we were having to start over (in 1988) with my back to the wall. This couldn't be bigger."

There have been other wins that were just as big — or bigger — in Ole Miss' tremendous tradition such as the 21-14 win over Maryland in 1952, a 20-13 win over Notre Dame in 1977 and a 21-19 upset of LSU in 1986.

Alabama had a 12-0 lead before blowing it. The loss cast a pale over Alabama coach Bill Curry, who was already being heavily criticized.

"There's really nothing to say about this game," Curry explained. "We got whipped. They shut us down offensively — literally we deserve what we got. We were not prepared."

The Tide did not complete a pass in the game — the first time since

134

Fullback Joe Mickles (41) rambles around left end for an 18-yard touchdown in the final 15 seconds to give the Rebs a 22-12 win.

Reb halfback Shawn Sykes (46) gallops for a 53-yard TD in the third quarter. He added a 12-yard TD run in the fourth quarter.

Shawn Sykes celebrates the second of his two touchdowns against Alabama.

a 14-7 win over LSU in 1971.

Ole Miss won today on defense.

"Our defense and the kicking game just never allowed them to pull us down," Brewer said after his team outgained the Tide, 259-172.

At halftime neither team had scored.

But that changed when Pierre Goode took the second-half opening kickoff 100 yards for a touchdown. It was the third kickoff returned against the Rebs for a touchdown in three straight games.

When the Rebs got the ball, quarterback Mark Young was pinned in the Reb end zone by Tide tackle Tommy Cole for a safety, which bumped the Tide's lead to 9-0.

After Murry Hill returned a punt 51 yards, Philip Doyle added a 21-yard field goal to give Alabama a 12-0 lead.

With 11:42 left in the third quarter, Ole Miss took over and owned the remainder of the game.

Sykes scored first for the Rebs with a 53-yard gallop against a stunned Tide defense with 5:26 left in the third quarter.

Sykes added his second touchdown came on a 12-yard run with 2:07 left in the game. Darron Billings' two-point run gave the Rebs a 15-12 lead.

"That was a gutty call," Brewer said after the game, "and Red (Parker, the Rebs offensive coordinator) deserves all the credit. He called it. He called all of the plays."

The Rebs' final touchdown came on an 18-yard run around left end by fullback Joe Mickles, with 15 seconds left on the clock.

THE DIFFICULT YEARS

137

Ole Miss 42   Air Force 29

December 28, 1989 | Memphis, Tenn.

Reb's Speedy Takeoff Grounds Air Force in Liberty Bowl

Billy Brewer's Ole Miss Rebels blasted the Air Force back into orbit in their 42-29 win tonight before a record crowd of 60,128 in the Liberty Bowl. Reb quarterback John Darnell and Randy Baldwin led the Ole Miss attack. Darnell threw for 261 yards and a touchdown. Baldwin, the game's most valuable player, led Reb rushers with 177 yards and a pair of touchdowns.

Brewer's Rebs finished the season at 8-4 while Air Force wrapped up at 8-1.

Ole Miss' 42 points were the most ever in a bowl game. Their previous best was a 41-18 win over Georgia Tech in the 1971 Peach Bowl.

Prior to the game, the Ole Miss team received a visit from Chucky Mullins, who had been paralyzed during the season against Vanderbilt. The visit seemed to energize the entire team.

"We won the game for a great kid, Chucky Mullins," Brewer explained to the media after the contest.

Ole Miss scored on their first two possessions and had built a 28-9

Ole Miss	14	14	7	7 —	42
Air Force	9	0	6	14 —	29

lead by halftime.

Baldwin scored two of the touchdowns and had 121 yards rushing in this period. Darnell added a touchdown through the air and speedy Pat Coleman returned a punt 58 yards for a touchdown.

The opening touchdown came in 77 seconds on a 70-yard march. Darnell's 32-yard toss to flanker Reid Hines capped the scoring drive.

Air Force got on the scoreboard with a 37-yard field goal by Joe Wood.

Ole Miss' second touchdown came on a 7-play, 67-yard drive, with Baldwin sweeping right end for 23 yards and the touchdown to put Ole Miss up, 14-3.

Air Force rallied on a 62-yard drive that ended on a Dee Dowis 3-yard touchdown run to narrow the score to 14-9. A two-point con-

Randy Baldwin (24), the Liberty Bowl's MVP, led Reb rushers with 177 yards and two TD's.

Reb quarterback John Darnell (4) looks for a receiver downfield. Darnell passed for 261 yards and 1 TD against the Falcons.

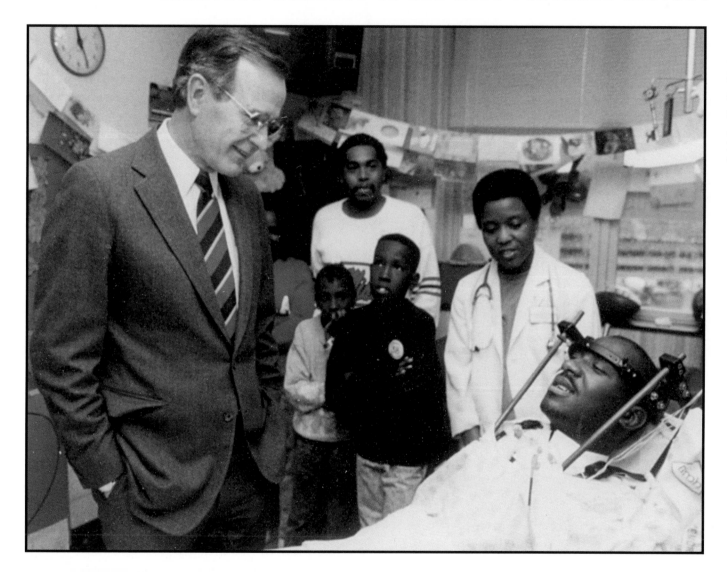

President George Bush visited with injured Reb defensive back Chucky Mullins prior to the Liberty Bowl.

THE DIFFICULT YEARS

version was intercepted by Reb safety Jeff Carter.

But this was the beginning of the end for the Falcons.

Carter later intercepted a Falcon pass and the Rebs scored in two plays. A 21-yard run by Baldwin cashed it in to give Ole Miss a 21-9 lead.

Coleman brought the crowd to their feet when he returned a Falcon punt and danced down the sideline for a touchdown.

Fisher DeBerry, the Air Force coach, summed up his team's embarrassing loss when he noted: "If you turn the ball over four times like we did, you're going to get beat."

141

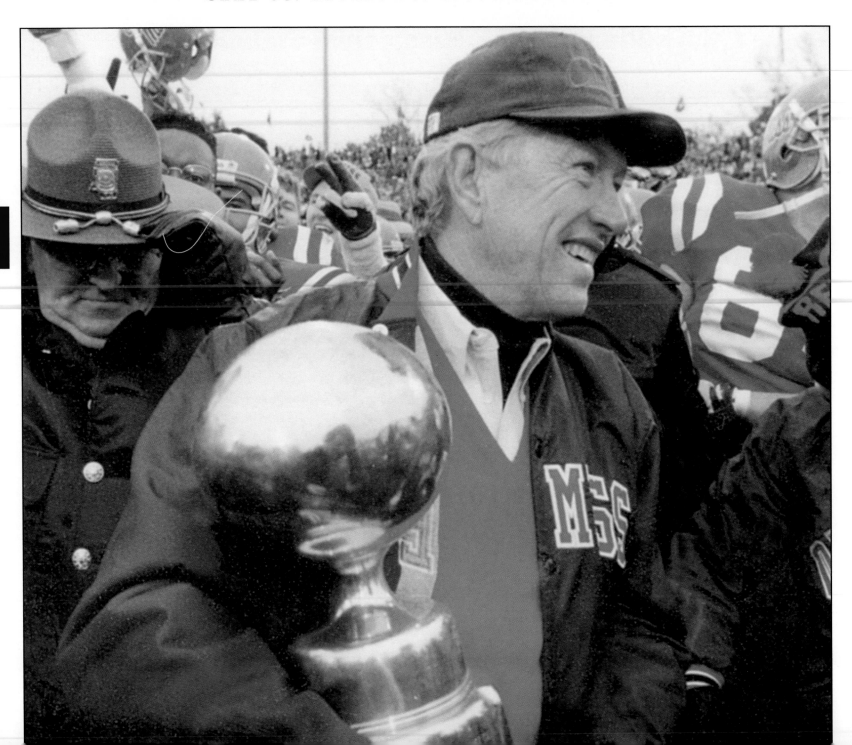

Ole Miss 17   Mississippi State 10

November 28, 1992 | Oxford, Miss.

Rebels' Defense Halts Bullies' Last-Minute Rally

The goalpost came down in the north end zone of Vaught-Hemingway Stadium today after Ole Miss stopped a pair of Mississippi State drives inside the Rebs' 10-yard line in the final three minutes. "I've never seen an effort like that by the guys in red shirts," said Ole Miss coach Billy Brewer."

The Bulldogs had 11 opportunities from inside the Reb 10-yard line in the last moments of this storied rivalry. They never were able to penetrate the Ole Miss defense.

Waiting for the winner was the Golden Egg Trophy which goes to the winner of this annual affair. A crowd of 41,500 was on hand, including several thousand with cowbells.

When the final buzzer sounded, Brewer was hoisted on top of his players' shoulders and given a ride to midfield. Ole Miss now leads the series with Mississippi State, 52-31-6.

Mississippi State only gained 39 yards on the ground against the stingy Rebel defense. Ole Miss made life even tougher for the Bulldogs

Mississippi State	0	10	0	0 —	10
Ole Miss	0	7	7	3 —	17

with four sacks and nine tackles for losses.

Yet with 54 seconds remaining, State was on the Reb 1 with second and goal. Then Chad Brown, the Reb tackle, found an opening in the State line and stopped Bulldog halfback Randy Brown for a 3-yard loss.

"I saw the guard getting ready to pull, and I knew what the play was going to be," Brown later explained.

The win over State earned Ole Miss an invitation to play Air Force in the Liberty Bowl on Dec. 31. Ole Miss has an 8-3 record and a four-game winning streak. The Rebs also finished second in the SEC Western division with a conference record of 5-3.

State fell to 7-4 and will be playing North Carolina State in the Peach Bowl on Jan. 2 in Atlanta. The Bulldogs finished with a 4-4 record in SEC play. This was their first visit to Oxford since 1972.

143

THE
DIFFICULT
YEARS

Cory Philpot (30), who led the Rebs with 994 yards rushing in 1992, scored on a 7-yard TD run in the third quarter.

"Any loss is bitter, but there's nothing you can do about it. It's great for the state to have this kind of rivalry," State coach Jackie Sherrill said after the game. "We had plenty of opportunities to win."

State led, 10-7, after a strange first half that saw the Bulldogs lose three fumbles and Ole Miss lose four fumbles and had two interceptions.

The Bulldogs' lone touchdown came in the second quarter. Ole Miss had been penalized for a personal foul on a 32-yard field goal that had been wide.

After the penalty had been levied, Michael Davis, the Bulldogs' fullback, rammed 7 yards for the touchdown. Garner's extra-point kick made it 7-0.

Gardner made it 10-0 on a 22-yard field goal with 8:20 remaining in the half. State had traveled to the Reb 5 before being stopped.

The Rebels got on the scoreboard after a State fumble by punt returner Tony James at the Bulldog 36. Ole Miss reached the State end zone in 3 plays.

Reb defensive tackle Chad Brown (88) stops State halfback Randy Brown's goal-line run in the final minute to preserve Ole Miss' 17-10 win.

THE
DIFFICULT
YEARS

145

Michael Lowery's interception of a Todd Jordan pass in the end zone with 2:27 left wrapped the win for the Rebels.

Defensive tackle Artis Ford drags down Bulldog fullback Michael Davis (37).

Quarterback Russ Snows hit fullback Marvin Courtney on a 7-yard pass for the touchdown. This narrowed the score to 10-7, with State ahead.

The Rebs scored late in the third quarter on a 7-yard run by Cory Philpot to give Ole Miss a 14-10 margin.

Brian Lee added a 22-yard field goal with 10:50 left in the game to boost the Rebs' lead to 17-10.

Philpot finished with 107 yards in the contest and 994 for the season.

Lee's field goal moved him into the leader spot on the Rebs' all-time scoring list.

THE DIFFICULT YEARS

Billy Brewer celebrates the win.

147

Ole Miss 15   Mississippi State 14

November 29, 1997 | Starkville, Miss.

Patridge Leads Rebs' Rally Against Bulldogs

"I t just can't get any better than this," said Ole Miss linebacker Walker Jones after the Rebels pulled off a dramatic 15-14 comeback win against archrival Mississippi State today. The Rebels began their final stretch run with 2:12 remaining and covered 64 yards in nine plays to narrow the Bulldogs' lead to 14-13. Stewart Patridge, the Rebs' quarterback, then tossed the game-winner to a diving Cory Peterson for the two-point conversion with 25 seconds left to give Ole Miss the victory.

"This is the kind of game you dream about as a kid," Patridge, the son of a former Bulldog halfback, explained in the locker room after the game.

Ole Miss is now 7-4 and hopeful for a bowl game.

But the cigar-smoking Rebs had their minds on other important items before the game. 45 minutes before kickoff the emotions between both teams erupted and a fight broke out near midfield. The players later blamed that the other team had been taking up too much room and loud taunting as reasons for the brawl.

| Ole Miss | 7 | 0 | 0 | 8 | — | 15 |
| Mississippi State | 0 | 7 | 7 | 0 | — | 14 |

The Rebels scored the first time they got the ball by traveling 71 yards in 13 plays. Patridge's 35-yard pass to wingback Andre Rone sealed the touchdown.

State evened the score at 7-all in the second quarter on a 5-yard pass from reserve quarterback Rob Morgan to tight end John Jennings.

The Bulldogs increased their lead to 14-7 in the third quarter when J.J. Johnson ripped through the line for a 1-yard TD. Johnson finished the season with 1,069 yards.

The game turned on a decision by Bulldogs coach Jackie Sherrill, who opted to have Brian Hazelwood kick a 52-yard field goal with less than three minutes remaining.

Sherrill later explained, "The decision I made was to go ahead and make them score twice."

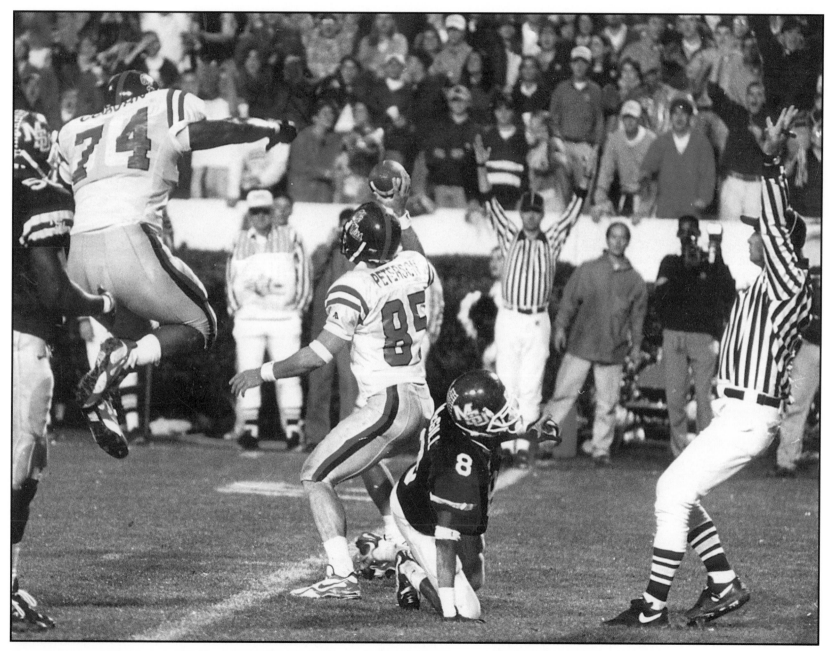

THE
DIFFICULT
YEARS

Cory Peterson (85), who caught five passes for 74 yards, celebrates his game-winning catch against the Bulldogs.

"They had to go 80 yards. You still got to make the plays."

Patridge and Ole Miss made the plays that counted, with the Rebs cashing in on the 10-yard pass to Rone.

Then came Ole Miss coach Tommy Tuberville's moment of decision.

THE DIFFICULT YEARS

"I changed my mind twice, but went with my first instinct to go for two," said Tuberville after the game. "But I saw the look in the offensive line's eyes and I couldn't deny them the chance ... I told them to go for it."

Peterson, who had caught five passes for 74 yards, cut across the middle and Patridge let loose a bullet.

"It was the biggest play of Stew's life — and maybe all of our lives," Peterson later recalled.

Moments later, Tim Strickland then ended any chance of a State comeback when he intercepted a Bulldog pass at the Ole Miss 25.

Stewart Patridge's 9-play, 64-yard drive in the final two minutes ensured the Rebs' win.

Ole Miss 34   Marshall 31

December 26, 1997 | Pontiac, Mich.

Patridge Leads Another Reb Rally Against Thundering Herd

THE DIFFICULT YEARS

Stewart Patridge, the Rebels senior quarterback who once gave up his football uniform to work on his father's farm, threw for three touchdowns in the second half to lead Ole Miss to a 34-31 comeback win over Marshall in the inaugural Motor City Bowl at the Silverdome.

The unranked Rebels (8-4) roared from a 17-7 halftime deficit to pull out the win.

Patridge was aided by the strong running attack of his tailbacks John Avery and Deuce McAllister.

The Rebels' final touchdown journey took nine plays and 75 yards and ended with a 1-yard blast by McAllister with only 31 seconds left.

It was the Rebels' second straight comeback win. They defeated archrival Mississippi State, 15-14, a few weeks earlier in the same manner.

"It's been like that with these guys all year," Ole Miss coach Tommy Tuberville explained after the game.

The Rebels had to score twice in the fourth quarter to win because

Ole Miss	7	0	14	13 —	34
Marshall	10	7	0	14 —	31

Marshall kept putting points on the scoreboard.

Patridge, who was voted Ole Miss' most valuable player in the game, completed 29 of 47 passes for 332 yards and three TD's. He had only one interception.

His counterpart, Marshall quarterback Chad Pennington, passed for 337 yards and three TD's while completing 23 of 45 attempts. He was tapped as Marshall's most valuable player.

After the contest, he noted, "It was just one of those games where the team that had the ball last didn't have enough time."

Marshall's fates were sealed when Rebel linebacker Broc Kreitz stripped the ball from all-America receiver Randy Moss at the Reb 26 with one second left.

Patridge marched Ole Miss on scoring drives of 59 and 75 yards in

151

THE
DIFFICULT
YEARS

Wide receiver Sheldon Morris (86) dashes upfield after a reception with a trio of Marshall defenders in pursuit.

Deuce McAllister (22) scored on a 20-yard TD pass and the game-winning 1-yard blast with only 31 seconds left.

the final quarter to overcome Thundering Herd leads of 24-21 and 31-27.

Ole Miss opened the game with Patridge flinging a 54-yard pass to Grant Heard. He was pulled down at the Marshall 1. Avery leaped the middle of line for the touchdown.

Marshall then responded with Pennington tossing a 80-yard bomb to Moss to tie the score at 7-7.

The play took only 11 seconds. Moss would finish the game with six receptions for 173 yards.

Avery ended up with 110 yards on 27 carries and McAllister had 71 yards on 8 carries.

McAllister also caught the 20-yard TD pass that gave Ole Miss a 21-17 lead in the third quarter..

Marshall's Billy Malaschevich booted a 36-yard field goal to give the Thundering Herd a 10-7 lead late in the first quarter.

Pennington threw a 19-yard pass to Herd flanker LaVorn Colclough to wrap-up a 44-yard drive to boost Marshall's lead to 17-7.

Ole Miss narrowed that lead to 17-14 when Patridge connected with wingback Andre Rone at the beginning of the second half.

"I think the whole difference in the game was that we were able to run the ball in the second half and we pretty much wore them down," Tuberville concluded.

THE DIFFICULT YEARS

RETURN TO GLORY

*"We were looking for a man with impeccable character, integrity and values ...
a proven coach, recruiter and leader of men. We wanted a person
committed to not take this job, but finish it."*

OLE MISS ATHLETIC DIRECTOR JOHN SHAFER

Ole Miss 35   Texas Tech 18

December 31, 1998 | Shreveport, La.

Cutcliffe's Rebs Upset Texas Tech in Independence Bowl

RETURN
TO
GLORY

An inspired Ole Miss team playing under new head coach David Cutcliffe was a winner tonight, 35-18, against Texas Tech in the 23rd Sanford Independence Bowl.

After the game, Cutcliffe told his team, "I've never been so proud of a football team than I am of you guys tonight."

The Rebels, who had lost their head coach and his staff when Tommy Tuberville left to take the head coaching job at Auburn, combined the Rebels' old playbook and the No. 1-ranked Tennessee Vols' system to produce a game plan that will be remembered by Ole Miss fans for a long time.

Romaro Miller, the Rebs' sophomore quarterback who had returned from a late-season collarbone injury, rewrote the Independence Bowl record books with his three-TD passing performance.

Cutcliffe, himself, had to overcome a 5-day stay in the hospital last week for pancreatis and a doctor's prognosis that he wouldn't be well in time to rejoin the Rebels for the bowl game.

Ole Miss	7	7	0	21	—	35
Texas Tech	7	3	0	8	—	18

But once they were together in Shreveport, Cutcliffe's team came to win.

Prior to the game, Cutcliffe told his team "to go out and win the physical war." The Rebels delivered.

Matt Luke, the Rebels' senior center, explained the reason for the team's success. "After that pregame speech Coach Cutcliffe gave, there was no way we were going to lose. He said that nobody was behind us except ourselves and our fans."

Romero put the Rebels in the lead for good at 21-10, with his 26-yard touchdown pass to Cory Peterson with 8:22 left in the fourth quarter.

The Rebels finished the scoring with a 43-yard run on an offside kick by Tech with 38 seconds left in the game.

Afterward, the Rebel players, who were aware of their coach's recent

Reb defensive end Robert Gates (99) chases after Texas Tech quarterback Matt Tittle (16) in the second half.

RETURN
TO
GLORY

CUTCLIFFE NAMED NEW REBELS' COACH

OXFORD, Miss., Dec. 2, 1998 — David Cutcliffe, the offensive genius who developed quarterbacks Andy Kelly, Heath Shuler, Peyton Manning and current Vol field general Tee Martin at No. 1-ranked Tennessee, was named head coach at Ole Miss today.

"We tried to get a real coach for real players," Ole Miss chancellor Robert Khayat explained. Forty years ago, Khayat was booming kicks on John Vaught's top-ranked Rebels, who were playing in New Orleans on New Year's Day each year.

Cutcliffe was hired four days after Rebel coach Tommy Tuberville bolted from Ole Miss to take the head coaching job at Auburn. Cutcliffe signed a contract worth $1.6 million — approximately the same Turberville got at Ole Miss.

"We were looking for a man with impeccable character, integrity and values ... a proven coach, recruiter, and leader of men," John Shafer, the Ole Miss athletic director explained. "We also wanted a person committed not to take this job, but finish it."

Cutcliffe arrived in Oxford last night, met with his team this morning and flew back to Knoxville in time for the Vols' practice leading up to this Saturday's SEC Championship Game against Mississippi State.

He will return to Oxford on Sunday to begin bowl preparations.

RETURN TO GLORY

Jamie Armstrong (7), the Reb wide receiver who is surrounded by a trio of Tech defenders, goes airborne to pull down a Romero Miller pass.

illness, dumped a Gatorade cooler filled with paper cups on him. They then carried him across the field on their shoulders.

Miller was voted the offensive player of the game and Kendrick Clancy was awarded the defensive player of the game. He finished the game with 7 tackles.

Ole Miss finished the season with a 7-5 record after losing three straight games.

The Rebels' dominance was due to an aggressive defense that shut down Ricky Williams, the fourth best running back in the country who had averaged 143.8 yards per game. He was held to 85 yards on 23 carries.

Reb halfback Deuce McAllister

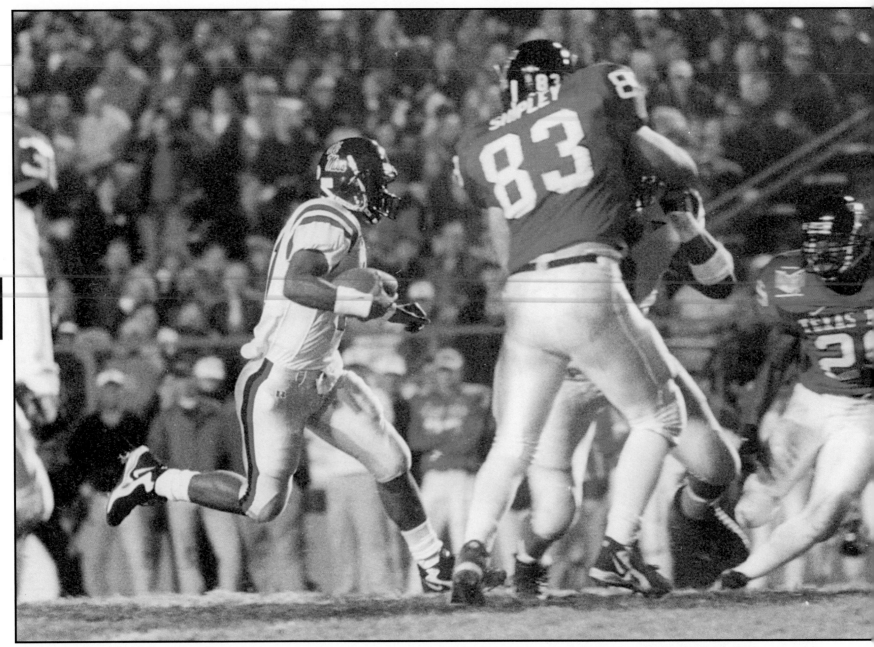

Ole Miss quarterback Romero Miller (11) returned from a late-season collarbone injury to lead the Rebs to a 35-18 victory.

A

Abdo, Nicholas, QB, 1927
Abide, Gary, LB, 1989-90-91-92-93 (co-c)
Ables, Winifred Wayne, mgr., 1980
Adamcik, Rich, OT, 1986; OG, 1987
Adams, Billy Ray, FB, 1959-60-61
Adams, John C., C, 1909-10-11-12 (c)
Adams, Lawrence A., Jr., QB, 1992-93;
    SS, 1995; HB, 1996 (co-c)
Adams, Robert O. (Tiger), E, 1952-53-54
Adams, Winfred C., sub-RG, 1908-09
Ainsworth, Stephen Gregory, TB, 1970-71-72
Akin, Wm. E. (Dooley), FB, 1921-22-23-24
Albritton, Sam, DT, 1984
Aldridge, John B., DT, 1968-69-70
Aldridge, Walter P. (Bo), T, 1962-63-64
Alexander, Alishma R., TB, 1997
Alexander, Charles H., Jr., mgr., 1972
Alexander, George E., E, 1920-21
Alexander, Jud, OG, 1983-84; OG-C, 1985
Alexander, Raymond M., DE, 1974
Alford, John Warner, LG, 1958-59-60 (co-c)
Alford, Neil H., TE-OG, 1995
Allen, Charles B., FB-QB, 1923-24-25
Allen, Elmer Dale, ST, 1969; DT, 1970-71
Allen, Herman Eugene, FB, 1971-72-73
Allen, John Franklin, G, 1981-82-83
Alliston, George B., G, 1966
Alliston, Vaughn S., Jr. (Buddy), LG, 1953-54-55 (c)
Ambrose, J. R., SE, 1984-85; FL, 1986-87
Ames, Charles F., C-T, 1901-02
Amos, Dwayne, WR-DB, 1988; RB, 1989;
    CB, 1990-91-92
Amsler, Guy, G, 1920
Anderson, Cephus, C, 1913-14; 1916 (c)
Anderson, James N. (Hoss), FB, 1958-59-60
Anderson, Vernon, mgr., 1941
Anding, Eli K., WB, 1994; UB, 1995; LB-UB, 1996; FB, 1997
Applewhite, Austin H., E, 1925-26-27 (c)
Armstrong, Crowell H., LB, 1969-70-71
Armstrong, George W., T, 1923-24
Armstrong, James H. (Jamie), WR, 1998
Armstrong, Johnny, DB, 1981-82-83-84
Armstrong, Tyji, TE, 1990-91
Arnette, J. W., T, 1944
Arnold, John Wes, Jr., mgr., 1966
Arnold, Robert P., LB, 1972; DE, 1973-74
Arrington, Perry, C, 1988-89
Ashford, Andre L., trainer, 1972
Ashley, Tyrone, SE, 1989; FL-DB, 1990; RB-DB, 1991
Aston, Vernon (Monk), C, 1935-36-37
Austin, Kent, QB, 1981-82-83-84-85
Austin, Oliver A., mgr., 1910
Autrey, Winkey, C, 1937-38-39
Avery, John E., RB, 1996-97 (co-c)
Ayers, Chris, mgr., 1989
Ayers, Richardson, C, 1908

B

Bacon, Jeff, LB, 1984-85-86

Bagwell, C. I., T, 1917-18
Bagwell, Michael Wm., WB, 1970
Bailess, Robert R. (Bob), LB, 1971-72-73
Bailey, James, TE 1993
Bailey, Jay Alan, LB, 1978
Bailey, Robert W., M, 1966-67-68 (co-c)
Bailey, William Jason, trainer, 1997-98
Baker, Jerry E., FB-RHB, 1954-55-56
Baker, Mark M. (Mitch), DT, 1997; OG, 1998
Baldwin, Randy, RB, 1989-90
Ball, John H., HB, 1914; 1916
Ball, Warren N. (Bo), E, 1958-59-60
Bane, Bob, mgr., 1977
Barber, John T., RH, 1954
Barbour, Calvin C., Jr., HB-QB 1919-20-21-22 (c)
Barfield, Kenneth A., T, 1950-51
Barker, Reuben A. (Rube), T, 1911-12
Barkley, William Donald, LE, 1955; 1957
Barlow, Bobby, trainer, 1985-86
Barlow, T. Michael, TB, 1974
Barnes, Blake, mgr., 1977
Barnes, Phillip E. (Gene), DT, 1996-97
Barnett, Eddie Lee, G, 1967
Barry, Wm. T. (Bill), FLK, 1971-72
Bartling, McNeil (Doby), QB, 1934-35
Basham, Wm. Earl, T-G, 1959-60-61
Baskin, John Frank, DT, 1969
Bates, G. C., RT-LG, 1905-06
Batten, H. C., FB, 1926
Battiste, Chris, OG, 1992
Baumsten, Herb, QB-FB, 1935-36-37
Beanland, Gayle C., QB, 1898-99; 1902
Beatty, Edwin M., C, 1951-52-53 (c)
Beck, John Robert, LB, 1976-77
Beckett, B. B., LE, 1901-02
Beckett, George B., LE, 1900
Beckett, Richard C., Jr., RE, 1905
Beddenfield, Marcus, E, 1934
Beddingfield, Wm. Ray, C, 1963-64-65
Bell, Jeffrey D., trainer, 1980
Bell, Jonathan (Jon), FB, 1992; DE, 1993
Bell, Tim, trainer, 1980-81-82
Bender, Charles A., FB, 1913-14
Bennett, Gardner, G, 1937
Bennett, James K. (Bo), DE, 1996; FB, 1997
Bennett, Preston (Pep), QB, 1940-41; 1946
Bennett, Tony (Gator), DE, 1986; NG, 1987;
    OLB, 1988-89 (co-c)
Bentley, M. C., G, 1929
Benton, Robert Hollis, RT, 1958-59-60
Benvenutti, Joseph D., DT, 1974
Berger, Andrew J. (Andy), WR, 1994
Bernard, Dave, FB-HB, 1934-35-36
Bernocci, Robert, T, 1940-41-42
Berry, Lance, K, 1992
Berry, O. L., mgr., 1925
Berryhill, Herman, E, 1934
Besselman, Jim, OG, 1986; OT, 1987
Bethay, Kenneth Lee, trainer, 1980
Bettis, Jeffery A. (Adam), TE, 1996-97-98
Bevill, Scott, mgr., 1988
Bidgood, Charles S., C, 1947-48

Biggers, Neal B., HB, 1929-30-31 (c)
Bigham, C. S., sub., 1908
Bilbo, G. W., E-G, 1931-32-33
Bilbo, J. P., G, 1935-36-37
Bilbrew, Damon A., WR, 1995-96
Biles, George Lacey, HB, 1924-25-26
Billings, Darron, FB, 1988; RB, 1990-91 (co-c)
Bingham, Dwight, DE, 1982-83-84
Bisbing, Willard, LH, 1938
Bishop, Clark D., E, 1949
Bishop, Smith, T, 1913-14
Black, Willis W., HB, 1954
Blackwell, Anse, E, 1938
Blackwell, Bernard, LG, 1944-45-46-47
Blair, Earl E., LHB, 1952-53-54-55
Blair, George L., LHB, 1958-59-60
Blair, Wiley S., sub., 1905
Blake, Walter G., RG, 1893-94
Blakemore, Robert E. (Bob), DE, 1980-81;
    DT, 1983-84 (co-c)
Blalack, Charley, mgr., 1956
Blalack, John W., QB, 1954-55-56
Blanchard, Reginald, mgr. (video), 1997
Blankenbaker, R. H., HB-G, 1926-27-28
Blount, Clayton, HB, 1946
Blount, Joseph L., LB, 1967-68-69
Blount, Kenneth Lloyd, S, 1970
Boatman, Johnny, FB, 1985-86
Bogard, Harold, E, 1935
Boggan, Rex Reed, RT, 1949-50; 1954
Bolden, Saud Paul, DT, 1997
Bolin, Treva (Bookie), RG, 1960-61
Bonds, Eldridge D. (Bubba), WR-Holder, 1993-94-95
Bonham, Vince, C, 1988-89
Bonner, Antonious D., FS, 1993-94
Bontrager, Thomas, trainer, 1984-85
Bookout, B. E., HB, 1917
Boone, James T. (Pete), C, 1970-71-72
Boone, Michael L., DT, 1996-97-98
Booth, Carl C, III (Cliff), MG, 1968
Boothe, R. V., sub., 1893
Bounds, Wayne Stanley (Stan), QB, 1973; 1975
Bourdeaux, R. H., sub., 1893
Bourne, Robert G, 1961
Boutwell, George, C, 1928-29-30
Boutwell, Jeffrey C. (Jeff), WR, 1995-96-97
Bowen, B. C., RT, 1898
Bowen, John H. (Buddy), Jr., QB, 1946-47-48
Bowen, John H., III (Bo), TB, 1967; FB, 1968-69 (co-c)
Bowen, Mark Sutton, SE, 1976
Bowens, Tim, DT, 1993
Bowers, Samuel H., QB, 1919
Bowles, Wallace C., T-G, 1929-30-31
Bowman, Gayle, HB, 1955
Boyce, Boykin, G, 1944-45
Boyce, Daniel, OG, 1983; LB, 1984-85
Boyd, Danny, CB, 1989-90-91-92
Boyd, Lucas, mgr., 1953
Boyd, Robert C. (Bobby), QB, 1962
Boykin, A. L. (Showboat), HB-FB, 1949-50-51
Bradley, Bruce B., LH, 1949-50
Bradley, Kimble, QB, 1936-37-38 (c)

Brady, T. P., LT, 1893
Brandon, Gary, mgr., 1978
Brandon, Ronnie, mgr., 1980
Brasher, Kristopher L. (Kris), trainer, 1995
Brashier, Rodgers, G, 1952-53-54
Breland, Hugh Gregory, P, 1973-74
Breland, Jesse J., FB-HB, 1912-13
Breland, R. Q., mgr., 1923
Brenner, George, FB, 1950-51-52
Brents, Darrell, C, 1944
Bressler, Arthur (Art), Jr., OG, 1971-72-73
Brewer, Brett, P, 1984
Brewer, Derek O., DB, 1980
Brewer, Grady, FB, 1945
Brewer, Jack, E, 1944
Brewer, Joe, G, 1982-83; LB, 1984; NG, 1985
Brewer, Johnny Lee, RE, 1957; 1959-60
Brewer, Homer (Billy), DB-QB, 1957-58-59
Breyer, Alex, G, 1934-35-36
Brice, Alundis, FS, 1991-92; CB, 1993; CB,1994 (co-c)
Bridgers, David I., C, 1946-47
Bridgers, David I., Jr., C, 1968; WG, 1969-70
Bridgers, Lloyd M., mgr., 1975
Bridges, James T., E, 1951-52
Bridges, Roy, QB, 1917 (c)
Briggs, Charles E., mgr., 1924
Brinkley, Lester, DT, 1985-86-87-88
Brister, Fred E., III, LB, 1968-69-70
Brister, Herndon, FB, 1930
Brister, Thomas S., RE, 1961
Britt, Alvin, C-G, 1931-32-33
Britt, Oscar, G, 1940-41-42
Broussard, Ken G., T, 1965
Brown, Allen, E, 1962-63-64 (co-c)
Brown, Alton L., DT, 1971-72
Brown, Burkes, OT, 1991-92
Brown, Carter, HB, 1952
Brown, Chad, DL, 1991-92 (co-c)
Brown, Colon, HB, 1929-30
Brown, Dean, SE, 1984; 1985
Brown, Ernest Herman, S, 1970; SLB, 1971
Brown, Fred, G, 1946
Brown, Jerry G., T, 1959-60-61
Brown, Melvin A., RB, 1979; CB, 1980-81-82
Brown, Patrick, LB, 1982-83-84-85
Brown, Raymond L., QB, 1955-56-57
Brown, Renard T., FB, 1992-93; DE, 1995 (co-c)
Brown, Stuart T., WR, 1995-96-97
Brown, Tim, OG, 1988-89 (co-c)
Brown, Titus, FL, 1986
Brown, Tony, OLB, 1990-91
Brown, Wm. Van, WB, 1967; KS, 1968
Brownlee, Vincent, WR, 1990-91
Bruce, John, QB, 1944-45
Bubrig, Eric S., C-OT, 1995-96
Buchanan, John P., DE, 1974
Buchanan, Oscar, T, 1944
Buchanan, Oscar W. (Red), QB, 1946-47-48
Buntin, R. R., G, 1915-16
Burford, Cecil, trainer, 1983-84
Burgess, Derrick L., DT, 1997; DE, 1998
Burgess, G. Bentley, DE, 1980

Burke, Charles G., Jr., LE, 1955; 1957
Burke, Jack, HB, 1931-32
Burke, Webster W., C, 1924-25-26 (c)
Burke, Robert O., Jr., WT, 1969-70; QT, 1971
Burkhalter, Charles Stephen (Steve), DT, 1971-72-73
Burleson, Charles, T, 1952
Burnett, Harvey, QB, 1930
Burnett, W. D. (Dump), T-G-FB, 1927-28-29 (c)
Burns, Willie, CB, 1977-78
Burrow, John D., DB, 1979-80-81; FS, 1982
Bush, Alan L., ST, 1965-66-67
Bush, Bill, OG, 1989; DL, 1991
Butler, George H., LG, 1900
Butler, James, G, 1944
Byrd, Ronard K. (Rocky), QB, 1949-50-51

C

Caccamo, Dan, SS, 1977-78-79
Cage, Charlie, Jr., DT, 1976-77-78
Cagle, Brian, DT, 1988; DE, 1989; DT, 1990
Cagle, Robert, OG, 1987
Cahall, William C., JR, 1911
Cain, George, FS, 1977
Cairnes, George H., sub., 1899-1900
Caldwell, David, FS, 1985; SE, 1987
Caldwell, James T., LG, 1950-51-52
Caldwell, M. F., T, 1917
Calhoun, Bill, trainer, 1984-85
Calicchio, Lawrence R. (Lonny), P-K, 1994-95
Callahan, Lindy T., HB, 1949-50-51
Campanova, Joseph F., KS, 1980
Campbell, David, DB, 1977
Campbell, Eugene P., RG-mgr., 1898 (c),1899
Campbell, Henry A., G, 1948
Campbell, Jeff, T, 1982-83
Campbell, J. W., FB, 1916
Campbell, Keith L., CB, 1992-93-95; SS, 1994
Campbell, William Mike, E, 1945
Cannion, Anthony E. (Tony), RB, 1996-97-98
Cannon, Glenn D., S, 1967-68-69 (co-c)
Cannon, Zachary H. (Zach), mgr., 1998
Cantrell, James Larry, OT, 1975
Cantu, Lorenzo (Herkey), OG, 1992
Capello, Harry, C, 1940
Carlisle, Wm. Todd, mgr., 1968
Carlson, Cully, E, 1935
Carlton, John, DT, 1985; 1987
Carmichael, Sidney J., DE, 1993-94
Carnes, Robert Lee, E, 1916
Carney, A. B., QB, 1918-19
Carpenter, Charles W. (Chuck), OG, 1971
Carpenter, Preston Caswell, TE, 1969; DE,1970-71
Carpenter, Terry Carol, WB, 1967
Carr, Oscar E, 1914
Carruth, Bert, FS, 1991-92
Carruth, Lester, G, 1932-33-34
Carter, Fred S., LG-T, 1909-10-11
Carter, Jeff, DB, 1988; FS, 1989-90-91 (co-c)
Carter, Raymond, G, 1965
Carter, Sam P., G-C, 1929-30
Carter, W. Spinks, C, 1901

Case, Harry, E, 1956
Casey, Johnathan C., OG, 1994-95-96
Casper, Raymond, QB-HB, 1931-32-33
Castle, C. E., HB, 1945
Castle, Lee, FB, 1941
Castle, Richard, HB, 1945
Caston, Hunter B., SS, 1996
Caston, Lester B. (Brent), TB, 1964; M, 1965-66
Causey, J. B., LT-G, 1909-10-11
Causey, Jimmy, S, 1971; QB, 1972
Cavin, Jack Ottis, RE, 1958
Chamberlain, D. H., LH, 1904
Champion, James E., HB, 1957-58-59
Champion, Wm. L. (Billy), LE, 1960; 1962
Chandler, John Caroll, LB, 1970-71-72
Chandler, Kyle, RH, 1899
Cheatham, Jack, G, 1945
Childers, Charles, P, 1987-88-89-90
Childres, Robert D., HB, 1952-53
Childs, Gregory L. (Greg), DT, 1994-95
Chisholm, Charles P., TB, 1964
Chisolm, Richard, P, 1991-92
Christian, Charles D., Jr., RH, 1907
Chumbler, Brent S. (Shug), QB, 1969-70-71
Chunn, Clifton B. (Cliff), Jr., DHB, 1968
Churchwell, Hanson (Bull), RG-T, 1957-58
Clancy, Lukendrick T. (Kendrick), DT, 1998
Clapp, Robert P., QB, 1899
Clark, Bobby, OG, 1982-83-84-85
Clark, James H., T, 1944; 1947-48-49
Clark, Marcus R. (Mark), FLK, 1976
Clark, Roger Lamar, DB, 1981-82-83
Clark, Wesley F. (Wes), mgr. (video) 1997
Clay, Wm. F. (Bill), WB-DHB, 1963-64-65
Cleveland, Chuck, TB, 1985; FB, 1986-87
Clingan, Jason L., FS, 1996-97
Clippard, Richard F., OG, 1973-74; MG, 1975
Coates, David Patrick, QB, 1976-77
Cobb, Shawn, LB, 1987-88-89-90 (co-c)
Coburn, Devon K., DT, 1995; OT, 1996-97
Cohen, Sollie, FB, 1925-26-27
Cohn, Abye A., HB, 1901; 1903-04
Cohn, Henry L., RG-Mgr., 1909-10-11-12
Coker, Wm. H. (Billy), WB, 1968-69-70
Cola, Chris W., OG, 1995; DT, 1996
Cole, Alfred Lee, LB, 1980-81-82-83
Cole, Eddie Lee, LB, 1975-76-77-78
Cole, Milton R. (Hoppy), NG, 1980; G, 1981-82
Cole, Ryan, trainer, 1997
Coleman, Dennis F., DE, 1968-69-70 (co-c)
Coleman, Kem T., LB, 1974-75-76-77
Coleman, Pat, FL, 1988-89 (c)
Coleman, Ronald Justin, DB, 1998
Coleman, Roy, FLK, 1977; QB, 78-79
Collette, Allen, G, 1914-15
Collier, Antonio (Tony), FS, 1992; CB, 1993
Collier, James W., 1895
Collier, John Brooks, DT, 1969
Collier, O. E., HB 1926
Collier, Terry Lee, QB, 1967
Collier, William C., sub., 1893
Collins, Dudley, mgr., 1931

Commiskey, Charles E. (Chuck), C., 1977; 1979; OG, 1980
Conerly, Cecil L. III (Tank), mgr., 1977
Conerly, Cecil L. A. (Charlie), LHB, 1942;1946-47 (c)
Conlee, Clint, OT, 1990-91-92-93 (co-c)
Conn, Abe H., FB, 1898; 1901
Conner, Clyde R., T, 1902; 1906
Conner, Edgar E., RT, 1901
Conroy, James, HB, 1944
Cook, Casey, trainer, 1997-98
Cook, Richard, HB, 1925
Cook, Steven Chad, LB, 1997-98
Cook, William Henry, FB, 1893-94 (c)
Cooper, Allan, trainer, 1993
Cooper, Charles, T, 1945
Cooper, Harold, LG, 1956-57-58
Cooper, Kevin J., P, 1996-97
Cooper, Kyle M., LE, 1907
Correro, Van Sam, OG, 1973-74
Cothren, Jennings Paige, FB, 1954-55-56
Cottam, Chris C., OT, 1978-79-80 (co-c)
Courtney, Marvin, RB, 1990-91-92-93
Cowan, John Kuhl, RT, 1893-94
Cowan, R. C., RT, 1901
Coward, Charles B., LB 1967
Cowart, E. M., E, 1917-18-19 (c)
Cox, Owen E., G, 1950
Craddock, Benjamin A. (Ben), P, 1998
Craddock, Tyler J., LB, 1996
Crain, Charles K. (Ken), mgr., 1994-95
Crain, Milton, C, 1956-57-58 (co-c)
Crain, Sollie M., T-G, 1921-22-23-24
Crawford, Edward S. (Eddie), III, LHB, 1954-55-56
Crawford, James A., RG, 1946-47-48-49
Crawford, Othar A. Jr., LG, 1947; 1949-50-51 (c)
Creekmore, Rufus H., T-C, 1918-19-20 (c)
Creel, Jennifer, trainer, 1997
Crespino, Robert (Bobby), RHB, 1958-59-60
Crisman, William O., LH, 1900-01-02
Critz, F. A., Jr., RH-LH, 1900; 1902
Crocker, W. David, TE, 1974
Crook, G. W., FB, 1920
Crook, Jerry, HB, 1945
Crosby, William F. (Buddy), HB, 1961-62
Crowder, Talbert, T, 1937
Crowe, Dorman, C, 1938
Crull, Luther P. Jr. (Putt), MG, 1968
Cummins, Anthony, trainer, 1997
Cunningham, Julian D. (Doug), TB, 1964; WB, 1965; TB, 1966 (co-c)
Cunningham, James W., LH-sub., 1905-06
Cunningham, Stephen Vincent (Steve), RB, 1981; CB, 1982; FL, 1983; CB, 1984
Curd, H. P., mgr., 1919
Curland, Marvin, FB, 1946
Curlee, F. M., RG, 1900
Curtis, Chester, HB, 1932-33-34
Curtis, J. E., HB, 1915

D

Dabbs, Willis N. (Woody), RE, 1960-61-62

Dale, Roland H., C, 1945; T, 1947-48-49 (c)
Dalton, Andy, trainer, 1988-89-90
Dalton, Anthony D. (Tony), DT, 1979-80; G, 1981-82
Daly, Jerome, HB, 1942
Daniel, Josh, trainer, 1997-98
Daniels, Jerry S., E, 1958-59-60
Dantzler, Larry D., LB 1974-75; DE, 1976; LB, 1977
Darby, Al, trainer, 1982
Darnell, John, QB, 1987-88-89 (co-c)
Davenport, Butch, DB, 1985; CB, 1986-87; FS, 1988
Davidson, J. W. (Wobble), E, 1939-40-41 (co-c)
Davidson, P.G., E, 1919-20
Davis, Curtis Reed, LE, 1961-62-63
Davis, Edwin D., T, 1929-30
Davis, Frank, HB, 1945
Davis, Frank O., RHB, 1900
Davis, Harry, HB, 1949-50
Davis, J. E., E, 1923-24
Davis, Lee Andrew, CB, 1981; 1983-84
Davis, Mark, mgr., 1983
Davis, Paul, C, 1942; 1946
Davis, Richie, NG, 1986-87
Davis, Robert, T, 1924-25-26
Davis, Shed H., T, 1921-22-23-24
Dawson, D. A., HB, 1915
Day, Charles, T, 1940
Day, Herman (Eagle), QB, 1953-54-55
Day, William Glynn, LCB, 1976-77-78
Dean, Guy D., FB, 1901-02
Dean, William. J. (Joe), LT, 1962-63-64
Dear, W. C., HB, 1913; 1915
Dearie, Steven Patrick, TE, 1981
Deaton, Daniel B. (Penny), SE, 1969
Denmark, Eric, T, 1983-84
Dennis, Walter M. (Mike), TB, 1963-64-65 (co-c)
Denny, Billy, TE, 1977-78-79
Dent, Edward L., RG, 1903
Dentley, Tony, FB, 1986
Desler, Jonathan L. (Johnny), CB, 1993; 1995; FS, 1996
Dew, Cliff, C, 1990-91
Dickens, Luther (Curley), T, 1934-35-36
Dickerson, Cecil R., HB, 1946
Dickerson, David L., E, 1952-53-54
Dickey, Bubba, LB, 1985-86-87; OG, 1988
Dickson, Donald, RG, 1960-61-62
Diley, Brian V., mgr., 1998
Dill, John Reginald (Reggie), LB, 1970; DE, 1971-72 (co-c)
Dill, Kenneth D. (Kenny), C, 1961-62-63 (co-c)
Dillard, Wilson Jr., HB, 1950-51-52
Dillingham, Bruce, Jr., DHB, 1965-66-67
Dixon, Johnny, CB, 1990; SS, 1991-92-93 (co-c)
Dodd, Allen P., LG-LT, 1902-03-04-05 (c)
Dodson, Leslie, HB-FB, 1938-39-40
Dongieux, Paul A., LB, 1969-70-71 (co-c)
Dorrah, Clinton E., G, 1913
Dossett, Horace, T, 1938-39-40
Dotson, Albert C., CB, 1976-77
Dotson, Dewayne, LB, 1992-93 (co-c)

Dotson, G. Kenneth, DT, 1980-81-82
Dottley, John (Kayo), FB, 1947-48-49-50
Doty, Arthur W., LH, 1960-61
Dowell, Wade, C, 1977
Downing, Henry M., sub., 1903
Doyle, L. A., 1918
Drewry, Robert G., 1953-54-55
Dubuisson, Gene H., C, 1953-54-55
Duck, Charles E., G, 1955-56
Duke, John Gayle, QB, 1894
Dunagin, Charles Ado, T, 1937-38-39
Dunaway, James K. (Jim), RT, 1960-61-62
Duncan, Derek, mgr., 1983-84
Duncan, Sam, trainer, 1978
Dunlap, William E. (Ted), trainer, 1998
Dunn, Perry Lee, QB, 1961; FB, 1962; QB, 1963
Dunn, Thomas, HB, 1931
Durfey, Allan P., HB, 1918
Dykes, Jewell Kenny, Jr., mgr., 1968

E

East, F. J., G, 1915
Easterling, Jay, KS, 1979
Easton, Mike, OT, 1989
Edwards, Arthur M., trainer, 1975
Edwards, Xavier Omar, OT, 1995; OG-OT, 1996-97
Elam, Shane F., DE, 1998
Ellis, Timothy L. (Tim), QB, 1974-75-76-77
Elmer, Frederick W., RE-RH-mgr., 1900, 1901
    (c), 1902, 1903 (c), 1904
Elmer, James C., RT, 1906
Elmore, James Douglas (Doug), QB,
    1959-60- 61(co-c)
Elmore, J. W., 1924
Embry, Joseph S. (Joey), OT, 1996
English, Gino D., FLK, 1980-81-82
Enoch, Eugene S., QB-sub., 1900-01-02
Enochs, W. B., C, 1926-27
Epting, John Booth, HB, 1922
Erickson, W. C. (Bill), T, 1946-47 (alt-c)
Erves, Dale V., LB, 1979-80; FB, 1981
Erves, James C., DT 1979-80
Erwin, Clay, DE, 1977; 1980-81
Estes, Hermon Donald, mgr., 1964
Estes, Terry, mgr., 1970
Etua, Daniel, trainer, 1997
Eubanks, Bill, LE, 1940-41
Eubanks, Oscar G., 1921
Evans, David L., NG, 1993; OG, 1994; DT, 1995-96
Evans, Guy E. (Butch), QB, 1974; DE, 1975
Evans, Harrison, G, 1916
Evans, J. P. (Joe), E-QB, 1912-13-14
Ewell, Todd, mgr., 1997-98

F

Fabris, Jon Michael, FS, 1976-77; CB, 1978-79
Fabris, Robert S., TE, 1975; SE, 1976-77
Fagan, Julian W., III, P, 1967-68-69
Fair, Davis L., LG, 1901
Fair, Frank L., LE, 1903

Fair, Gene, mgr., 1937
Fant, Frank C., G, 1947-48-49
Farber, Louis A. (Hap), SE, 1967; DE, 1968-69
Farish, William S., RT-FB, 1899
Farmer, C. E., G, 1918-19
Farmer, Fred R., DHB, 1968-69-70
Farmer, James J., T, 1966-67
Farragut, Kenneth D., C, 1947-48-49-50 (c)
Farrar, Donald H. (Don), QB, 1968; 1970
Farris, Wm. J. (Bill), DE, 1973-74-75
Fedric, Jones, mgr., 1932
Feemster, J. H., T, 1919-20; 1922
Felts, Morris Leon, TB, 1968-69; SE, 1971
Ferguson, David, trainer, 1988-89
Ferguson, Troy M. (Huck), NG, 1993-94
Ferrill, Charles, C, 1931
Ferrill, Charles B., RT, 1960
Fields, Jimmy, NG, 1985
Fields, Richard J., HB, 1917
Finger, William, G, 1915
Finley, James A., FB-QB, 1904-05
Fischer, David M. (Danny), FLK, 1976
Fisher, Bobby F., LE, 1954-55
Fisher, Lasilas Comone, DL, 1996-97-98
Fisher, Ta'Boris L., WR, 1993; WB, 1994;
    HB, 1995-96
Fitzsimmons, Mike, NG, 1983; DT, 1984-85-86
Flack, Jackie, LH, 1940-41
Flakes, Everett, DB, 1984; SS, 1985-86
Fleming, Gordon W., Jr. (Rocky), RE, 1964;
    MM, 1965; WB, 1966
Fletcher, Ralph E., QB, 1912
Fletcher, Robert J., E, 1947-48-49-50
Fletcher, Spence, trainer, 1988-89
Flournoy, Maurice L., HB, 1998
Flowers, Charles (Charlie), FB, 1957-58-59 (co-c)
Flowers, Jesse, T, 1931-32-33
Follett, Michael J. (Mike), mgr., 1993-94-95
Foose, Sam, E, 1935
Forbes, George, trainer, 1988
Ford, Artis, DL, 1990-91-92
Ford, Cecil A., RT, 1961-62-63
Forester, Michael W., C, 1974; DT, 1975-76
Fortson, Edward D. (Ed), DT, 1994-95
Foster, John M., LE-RH, 1898-99-1900-01-02 (c)
Foster, Willie, FLK, 1978
Fountain, Michael A., CB, 1978-79-80
Fourcade, John, Jr., QB, 1978-79-80-81
Fourcade, Keith J., LB, 1979-80-81-82
Fowler, Ronald M. (Ronnie), C-G, 1964-65-66
Fox, Otis T., DE, 1995
Foxworth, T. J., QB, 1893
Frame, J. S. (Buntin), DHB, 1965
Franklin, Bobby Ray, QB, 1957-58-59
Franks, Floyd W., SE, 1968-69-70
Franks, Michael Dwayne, TB-SE, 1970; DHB, 1971
Fraser, D. R., mgr., 1928
Fratesi, Michael L. (Mickey), S, 1971;
    M, 1972; SS, 1973
Freightman, Phil, S, 1978-79
French, Rufus J., TE, 1996-97-98
Friedrichsen, Mark, T, 1982-83

Frishman, Leon B., mgr., 1967
Frye, J. P., G, 1940-41
Frye, William, FB, 1937
Fuerst, Robert J., G, 1946; 1948-49
Fulton, Lyman A., mgr., 1981
Funderburk, Joe, T, 1915
Furlow, Frank, QB, 1940

G

Gaddis, Jack T., HB, 1913
Galey, Charles D., E, 1945-46-47
Gallik, Gerald, OT-C, 1985, OT, 1986
Gardner, Thomas, mgr., 1938
Gardner, William P., G, 1919
Gardner, Wm. Douglas, G, 1932
Garner, Ernest L., Jr. (Lee), FB, 1964; LB, 1965-66
Garner, John C., Jr., DE, 1968
Garner, Robert L. (Bobby), QB, 1976-77-78 (c)
Garnett, C. L., 1895
Garrigues, Robert M., DHB, 1966-67-68
Gartrell, J. E., LT, 1900
Gary, Oscar Knox, Jr., LG, 1951-52
Gates, Hunter, G, 1946
Gates, Robert, W., DE, 1997-98
Gatlin, Todd E., KS, 1980-81-82
Gazelle, J. J., HB, 1922
Gebbia, Rich, TE, 1988-89
Genovese, Ross, OT-C, 1984-85
George, Alonzo P., G-HB, 1917; 1919-20
Gerrard, Albert L., Jr. (Bud), C, 1945; 1949
Gibbs, Jerry D. (Jake), QB, 1958-59-60 (co-c)
Gibson, E. B., 1895
Gibson, Jonathan, OG, 1992
Gilbert, Kline, E-T, 1950-51-52 (co-c)
Gill, Virgil, T, 1932-33-34
Gilliland, John L., DE, 1968-69-70
Gilruth, I. Newton, LE-RT, 1899-1900
Gipson, Malvin, TB, 1978; DB, 1979; TB, 1980-81
Gladding, Charles, E, 1939
Glover, Will H., LH, 1947
Gober, Oscar, 1921
Godwin, Chauncey, DB, 1988; CB, 1989-90-91
Goehe, Richard, RT, 1953-54-55
Goff, Rob, C, 1986-87
Goodloe, Willie, TB, 1984-85-86-87
Goodwin, Arthur, LE, 1940
Gordon, Craig, mgr., 1982
Gordon, J. Otis, G, 1919
Gordon, Louis, LB, 1988; OLB, 1989; TE, 1990
Gordon, Roger, FB, 1977
Gourley, John J., trainer, 1991-92-93-94
Graeber, Jerry B., SS, 1992; FS, 1993;
    FS, 1994 (co-c)
Graham, Bonnie Lee (Country), E, 1936-37-38
Graham, Darryl E., P, 1980-81-82
Graham, Korey, D., CB, 1997
Graham, Michael F. (Mike), SE, 1965
Grant, Roy Oliver, OG-T, 1975; OG, 1976
Grant, Walter G., K, 1993-94
Grantham, James Larry, LE, 1957-58-59
Graves, Joe E. (Jody), QB, 1965-66

Graves, Sam Ervin, III, LB, 1966-67
Gray, Brad, P, 1991-92
Gray, Dabney, mgr., 1969
Green, Allen L., C, 1958-59-60
Green, Jonathan, CB, 1991
Green, Marcus, DT, 1982-83-84
Green, Norvin E., C, 1900
Green, Randall W., P-K, 1996-97
Green, Walter G., HB, 1912
Green, Willie, WR, 1986-87; SE, 1988-89
Greene, James M., Jr., MG, 1979
Greenich, Harley, HB-FB, 1940; 1942
Greenlee, Max H., LT, 1964
Greenlee, Phillip Murry, FS, 1973
Grefseng, Robert Leonard (Bob), DE, 1976-77-78
Gregory, George H., Jr., E, 1958
Gregory, John Andrew, OT, 1970-71-72
Grice, Lashane T. (Shane), OL, 1998
Griffin, J. A., HB-E, 1914-15
Griffin, Malikia D., CB, 1994; 1996-97
Griffin, Wade H., OT, 1973; TE, 1975-76 (co-c)
Griffin, William K., KS, 1976
Griffing, Glynn, QB, 1960-61-62 (co-c)
Grigg, Jack Norwood (Woody), DT, 1979-80
Gryder, Robert L., trainer, 1978
Gunn, Edgar Lindsey, mgr., 1972
Gunn, Joe L., RB, 1998
Gunn, Lundy R., TE, 1973-74
Gunter, Bubba, OLB 1988-89
Gunter, George, FB-HB, 1932-33-34
Guy, Louis B., WB, 1960-61-62 (co-c)

H

Haddock, James W., S, 1965; 1967
Haik, Joseph Michel (Mac), SE, 1965-66-67 (co-c)
Halbert, Frank R., RH-FB, 1960-61
Hall, Gary S., Jr., 1972; RCB, 1973; FS, 1974
Hall, J. J., 1921
Hall, J. P., LT, 1899
Hall, James S., LH, 1957-58-59
Hall, Joe, DB, 1982-83
Hall, Linus Parker, HB, 1936-37-38
Hall, Wm. Whaley, LT, 1961-62-63 (co-c)
Hamilton, William F. (Bill), RCB, 1976
Hamley, Douglas (Doug), T, 1946-47, 1948 (c); 1949
Hamley, Stuart Douglas, Jr., TB, 1973
Hancock, Roger, SS, 1987; DB, 1988; SS,
    1989; OLB, 1990
Hand, Norman L., DT, 1993-94
Hannah, Otis, 1928
Hapes, Clarence, T-FB, 1934-35-36
Hapes, Merle, FB, 1939-40-41
Hapes, Ray, HB, 1935-36-37
Haralson, M. Flint, G, 1912
Harbin, Leon C. (Buddy), Jr., E, 1954-55-56
Harbour, James E., SE, 1980-81; FL, 1982; 1984
Harbuck, Sonny, OG, 1985-86-87
Harden, Edwin D., mgr., 1973
Hardin, Josh C., trainer, 1995
Hardy, Wm. H., Jr., sub., 1903
Harmon, Michael, FLK, 1979-80-81-82

Harper, Anthony Keith (Tony), TE, 1981-82
Harper, Brian, DL, 1991
Harper, Everette L., E, 1945-46-47
Harris, Antonio (T-Bird), TB, 1985
Harris, Dan D. (Danny), Jr., DHB, 1971; 1973
Harris, David, DL, 1991-92-93
Harris, George, E, 1952-53-54
Harris, I. H., FB, 1912
Harris, J. Harley (Pop), FB-T, 1913-14-15 (c)
Harris, James E., FB, 1974-75
Harris, Luther C. (Luke), DE, 1976
Harris, Pete, LB, 1988-89-90-91
Harris, R. S., mgr., 1916
Harris, Tony, DB, 1988
Harris, Wayne Stanley, WB, 1964
Harrison, Andre L., DE, 1996-97
Harrison, Elvin Lee (Harry), S, 1971-72-73
Harrison, Glenn D., MG, 1968
Harrison, Lance R., TE, 1995
Hart, Frank E., T, 1936-37-38
Hart, Granville W., LH, 1950
Harthcock, Billy Harold, WB, 1966-67
Hartzog, Hugh Miller, Jr., MG, 1967-68; DT, 1969
Harvey, Addison, LH, 1899
Harvey, Fernando C., LT, 1976-77-78
Harvey, James B., RT, 1963-64-65
Hatch, Johnny A., CB, 1974
Hathcock, Lance, DG, 1984-85; NG, 1986
Hathorn, Samuel C., LE, 1909-10
Havard, Gerald W. (Scooter), FB, 1969-70
Havard, Richard J. (Rickey), TB, 1969-70-71
Hawkins, James H. (Jimmy), OT, 1977-78-79
Hawley, Mike, mgr., 1984
Haxton, R. Kenneth, QB-HB, 1909-10; 1912
Haynes, Kirk, HB, 1930-31-32
Hazel, Homer Lawrence (Larry), G, 1939-40-41 (co-c)
Hazel, William (Billy), T, 1939-40-41
Head, Paul J., QB, 1993-94-95-96
Heard, Grant O., WR, 1996-97-98
Heard, Ronnie E., SS, 1996-97; LB, 1998
Heidel, James B., S-QB, 1963-64-65
Heidel, Herlan Ray, DHB, 1968-69-70
Heidel, Roy E., LE, 1963-64-65
Hemphill, Archie W., T-G, 1927-28
Hemphill, Robert E., HB, 1948-49
Hendrix, Robert E., Jr., WT, 1965; WG 1966; WT, 1967
Hendrix, Steven M., TE, 1980; G, 1981; FB, 1983
Henley, Tracy, trainer, 1982
Henry, Antonio, LB, 1990
Henry, Patrick, Jr., RE, 1898-99
Henry, Robert B., OG, 1975-76
Henson, Erwin D., E, 1916
Herard, Claude D., DT, 1967-68-69
Herman, Alvin J., DE, 1993-94
Herring, David, C, 1990-91
Herring, Stephen C., G, 1979; C, 1980-81-82
Herrington, Bart, C-E, 1931-32-33
Herrington, John C., sub., 1903
Herrod, Jeff, LB, 1984-85-86-87 (co-c)
Herron, Lee, trainer, 1991-92
Hervey, Tony, DT, 1990

Hester, S. D., G, 1929
Hewes, Gaston, 1924
Hickerson, Robert Gene, RT, 1955-56-57 (co-c)
Hickerson, Willie Wayne, RG, 1957
Hickman, James E., OT, 1973; OG, 1974; OT 1975
Hickman, Kendrick T., OT, 1996-97
Hicks, Rickye Allen, TE, 1972; FS, 1975-76
Hightower, C. C., sub., 1905-06
Hill, Jody, LB, 1990-91-92
Hill, Spencer C., mgr., 1998
Hill, Walter E. (Walt), HB, 1996; LB, 1997
Hindman, Stanley C., RG, 1963-64-65 (co-c)
Hindman, Stephen H., TB, 1966-67-68
Hines, Dexter D., LB, 1998
Hines, Reid, WR, 1986-87; FL, 1988-89
Hinton, Benjamin E., DE, 1975-76
Hinton, Charles R., C, 1964-65-66 (co-c)
Hinton, Cloyce M., KS, 1969-70-71
Hitt, Billy, C, 1951-52
Hofer, Paul D., FB, 1972-73-74-75 (tri-c)
Hoff, A. S., HB, 1923-24
Hoffman, Christian S., mgr., 1995-96-97
Hogue, Greg, P, 1987-88-89
Holcombe, James B., OG, 1991-92; OG-OT,1994
Holden, Allison, trainer, 1992
Holder, Jamie, FL, 1983; 1984 (co-c); 1985 (co-c)
Holder, Jeffrey, SE, 1988-89-90
Holder, Owen H., WT, 1968
Holladay, Robert, TE, 1987
Hollis, Andre T., WR, 1995
Holloway, A. J., Jr., HB, 1960-61-62
Holloway, Ernest D., E, 1913
Holston, William O., RG, 1900
Holston, John C., E, 1958
Hood, H. M., T, 1920
Hooker, Clyde, HB, 1944
Hooker, Danny L., S, 1968-69-70
Hooper, William K., Jr. (Kinny), FB, 1979-80; LB, 1981; RB, 1982
Hopkins, O. S., RG-FB, 1901-02
Hopkins, Thomas J., RG-LT, 1902-03
Hopson, Jay, FS, 1988; SS, 1989-90-91
Horn, Jeffrey L., MG, 1968-69-70
Horne, James H., LB, 1971; 1973
Horne, Steve, mgr., 1985-86
Hoskins, Danny, OG, 1984-85-86-87
Houchins, L. Larry, mgr., 1974
Householder, Eddy, LB, 1977-78-79
Hovater, Nobel Owen, RT, 1964
Hovious, John A. (Junie), HB, 1939-40-41
Howard, Jon, K, 1984-85
Howell, Earl O. (Dixie), HB, 1947-48
Howell, J. M., HB, 1920
Howell, L. F., T, 1918
Howell, Ray, Jr., E, 1950-51-52
Hoyd, William G. (Greg), LB, 1994
Hubbard, Ethelbert J., LH, 1898
Hubbard, Thomas Leon, LB, 1981-82-83
Huddleston, Quinnis (Fuzzy), LB, 1983-84-85-86
Hudson, Clark, 1979
Huff, Earl, T, 1955
Huff, Kenneth A., C, 1973

Huff, Tim, trainer, 1978
Huff, Walter W. (Bill), NG, 1980; SLB, 1981
Huggins, Cleveland P., RT-FB, 1904-05-06 (c)
Hughes, David, mgr., 1927
Humphrey, Arthur W., RB, 1981; FB, 1982-83-84
Humphrey, William R., G, 1950
Hunt, Kevin, mgr., 1988
Hurst, William Otis, FB, 1955-56-57
Hurt, Kevin, P, 1987
Hutchinson, James W., RE, 1898
Hutson, Earl, FB, 1932-33-34
Hutson, Marvin L., C, 1934-35-36 (c)

I

Ingram, James F., G-C, 1950-51-52 (co-c)
Ingram, Kevin, LB, 1990-91
Innocent, Doudow (Dou), RB, 1991-92; 1994-95 (co-c)
Inzer, William H., B, 1929
Ireys, Junius Taylor, HB, 1894
Irvin, Todd, TE-OT, 1984; OT, 1985-86-87 (co-c)
Irwin, Billy Carl, LE, 1962-63-64

J

Jabour, Robert, QB, 1948-49-50
Jackson, Abdul C., LB, 1991-92-93-94 (co-c)
Jackson, Antionne, DT, 1979
Jackson, Claude A. (Red), E, 1935-36
Jackson, Louis, DB, 1982
Jackson, Richard, LB, 1984
Jacobs, Doug, DT, 1988; DE, 1989; DT, 1990
James, Edward Thomas, Jr., DHB, 1965-66-67
James, James Elwyn, FB, 1969
James, Jerome P., G, 1913
James, Raymond L., LG, 1952-53-54
Jansen, Daniel J., RB, 1980-81-82
Janssen, William E. (Woody), OG, 1993-94
Jarman, Junius, 1924
Jarvis, Lewis Dewayne, TE, 1973-74
Jeanes, Kenneth L., DT, 1974
Jefcoat, Gregg, OG, 1978-79
Jenkins, Eulas S. (Red), FB, 1946-47-48-49
Jenkins, Robert L., QB, 1954
Jenkins, Warren D., RE, 1957-58
Jennings, David Sullivan, TB, 1962; 1964
Jennings, Steve, QB, 1977
Jennings, Thomas Wood, OT, 1975-76
Jernigan, Arthur F. (Skip), Jr., SG, 1968-69-70
Jernigan, Frank D., G, 1951-52-53
Jerome, Scott, OT, 1993
Jiggits, Louis M., HB, 1917; 1919
Johnson, Brandon B., trainer., 1996 -97
Johnson, Daren, FL, 1985; SE, 1986
Johnson, James L., C, 1901
Johnson, Joe C., E, 1944; 1947
Johnson, John, DT, 1977-78-79
Johnson, Larry Leo, WB, 1961-62-63
Johnson, Lawrence B., DT, 1974-75-77-78 (c)
Johnston, Hal G., RT-RG, 1907-08
Jones, Billy Ray, C-G, 1959-60-61 (tri-c)

Jones, Derek D., CB, 1993-94-95-96 (co-c)
Jones, Garland, RH, 1893
Jones, Gary M., FS, 1975-76-77
Jones, George F. (Buddy), WB, 1968-69-70
Jones, Hermit, T, 1942
Jones, Jerrell, QB, 1941-42
Jones, Johnny E., DE, 1994; 1996-97
Jones, Lopaz, DE, 1985-86-87; OLB, 1988
Jones, Robert H., G, 1928-29-30
Jones, S. M., LG, 1901
Jones, Walker W., III (Bill), TB, 1967; DHB, 1968-69
Jones, Walker W., IV, WR, 1994; SS, 1995; LB, 1996-97 (co-c)
Jones, William W., IV, (Bill), mgr., 1995-96-97
Jordan, James, MG, 1976-77-78-79
Jordan, Joel, OG, 1990-91-92-93
Jordan, William Roberts (Bill), TE, 1970; FLK, 1972
Joyce, Paul D. (Skip), C, 1993-94; OT, 1995
Joyner, Steve, TE, 1983-84-85-86
Joyner, William Seth, LB, 1996-97
Jumper, Zeke, E, 1927
Juneau, Donald C., K, 1998

K

Kanuch, Barry W., DE, 1978
Karliner, Randy, QB, 1992
Katzenmeyer, Fritz A., trainer, 1972
Kauerz, Don, T, 1945
Keaton, Grayson (Buster), G, 1921-22-23-24
Keith, John B., OL, 1998
Kelly, James A., FB-HB, 1951-52
Kemp, E. D., mgr., 1935
Kempinska, Charles C., RG-T, 1957-58-59
Kendall, Sam, C, 1915
Kennedy, Bryan G., DT, 1980; DE, 1981-82
Kent, Phillip, OLB, 1988-89-90-91 (co-c)
Kent, Robert W., mgr., 1972
Keyes, Jimmy Elton, MG-K, 1965-66; LB-K, 1967
Keys, David A. (Davey) ("Norm"), trainer, 1993-94-95
Khayat, Robert C. (Bobby), T-G-K, 1957-58-59
Killam, John, T, 1944
Killion, Curtis Bobby, C, 1996-97-98
Killion, Reed, LB, 1984-85
Kilpatrick, Wendell Terry, LB, 1972-73
Kimbrell, Fred T., Jr., C-LG, 1962
Kimbrough, Les, FLK, 1977-78
Kimbrough, Orman L., LE-LH-mgr., 1902-03; 1905
Kimbrough, Richard R. (Rick), FLK, 1973-74-75
Kimbrough, Thomas C., C, 1893-94
Kinard, Billy R., HB, 1952-53-54-55
Kinard, Frank M. (Bruiser), T, 1935-36-37 (c)
Kinard, Frank M., Jr., FB, 1962-63-64
Kinard, George, G, 1938-39-40 (c)
Kinard, Henry, G, 1938; 1940
Kincade, Robert, E, 1935-36-37
King, Derek, OG, 1986-87; OT, 1988
King, Derrick, LB, 1989-90-91-92
King, James, OG, 1986; OT, 1987; OG, 1988
King, Kenneth A. (Kenny), LB, 1973; 1974 (tri-c); 1975 (tri-c)

King, Michael L. (Mickey), C, 1969-70
King, Perry Lee, KS, 1968-69
King, Reagan L., P, 1997-98
King, Stark H., DE, 1966
Kinnebrew, Earl, RT, 1909-10
Kirk, Dixon, E, 1918
Kirk, Ken H., FB-C, 1957-58-59 (co-c)
Kirk, Robert D. (Bob), DE, 1976
Kisner, Donald, mgr., 1978
Kitchen, Boyd T., OT, 1993-94-95; OT-C, 1996-97
Kitchens, Donald Scott, SLB, 1976-77
Knapp, C. E., HB, 1927-28
Knight, John L., WR, 1994
Knight, William. R. (Bob), DHB, 1969; TB, 1970-72
Knott, David J., FS, 1994-95 (co-c)
Knox, Baxter N., LT, 1908
Knox, Ike C., LH-RH, 1907-08 (c)
Knox, William W., III, (Wally), DB, 1979-80-81-82
Kohn, Germaine, WR, 1991-92
Kota, Charles U. (Chuck), OG, 1975-76
Kozel, Chester, LT, 1939-40-41
Kramer, Larry E., TB, 1972-73-74
Kreitz, Broc P., RB, 1994; LB 1995-96 -97
Krell, Doug, C, 1944
Kretschmar, Wilson P., E, 1896
Kroeze, John, P, 1986
Kyzer, Sam, HB, 1929-30

L

Laird, Charles D., FB, 1960
Laird, Dewitt, C, 1928
Lake, R. H., HB, 1918-19
Lamar, Wayne Terry, LG, 1959-60
Lambert, A. C. (Butch), Sr., mgr.-trainer, 1948
Lambert, Franklin T. (Frank), P, 1962-63-64
Lambert, George R., T, 1946
Lane, Paul J., Jr., QB, 1980; CB, 1981; RB, 1982
Langley, Carl Edward, III (Hoppy), KS, 1976-77-78-79
Langston, Thomas E., T, 1950
Lanter, Lewis R., LE, 1961-62
Lantrip, Billy, OG, 1985
Lavinghouze, Robin C., KS, 1976-77
Lavinghouze, Stephen M., KS, 1972-73-74-75
Lawrence, Richard T. (Dick), OT, 1973; 1974 (tri-c); 1975
Lawton, Pat, HB-mgr., 1929-30
Lea, Jim, trainer, 1985-86
Lear, James H., QB, 1950-51-52
Lear, Jim, QB, 1977-78-79
Leathers, Don Wayne, OT, 1971; 1972 (co-c)
Leathers, W. S. (Dr.), mgr., 1902-03
Leavell, Leonard, RG-LG, 1907-08-15
LeBlanc, Allen Michael, DE, 1969-70-71
Lee, Alonzo Church, FB, 1908-09-10
Lee, Brian, K, 1989-90-91-92
Lee, Greg, TE, 1986-87
Leftwich, Frank M., E, 1921-22-23
Leftwich, George J., FB, 1912
Leggett, Chuck, trainer, 1978

Lenhardt, John, FB, 1937
Lentjes, Fred W., C, 1959-60-61
Lentz, Jim, DT, 1988; NG, 1989-90-91
Lester, Victor, OLB, 1989; NG, 1990
Letson, Ronald I. (Ronnie), HB, 1996; WR, 1998
Lewis, Carl, LB, 1980; DE, 1981-82-83
Lewis, Robert Q. (Bob), II, C, 1976-77
Lewis, Wm. Irwin (Buddy), C, 1966
Lillibridge, David B., E, 1916
Lilly, Sale T., HB, 1926-27
Lilly, T. J., HB, 1926
Lindsay, Derrick, FS, 1986-87
Lindsay, Everett, OT, 1989; OG, 1990-91; OT, 1992 (co-c)
Lindsey, Stephen K. (Steve), K, 1993; 1995-96-97
Lindstrom, Ricky, LB, 1984
Linton, Henry, Jr., T, 1951-52-53
Little, Jamie Ray, E, 1964
Little, Robert (Robbie), WR, 1991
Lloyd, Donald J., TE, 1978-79-80
Lockard, Walter W., sub., 1893
Lofton, Harol, HB-FB, 1951-52-53
Logan, Dameion, RB, 1991-92-93
Longest, Christopher C., LG, 1898-99-1900
Lorio, Franz, C, 1990-91-92-93
Lott, Billy Rex, RH, 1955-56-57
Lott, Lee, OT, 1988-89-90
Lotterhos, George T., DE, 1968-69-70
Loudermilk, Beth, trainer, 1997-98
Lovelace, Kent E., HB, 1957-58
Lovelady, Matthew, LB, 1980; DT, 1981; DE, 1982-83
Lowe, Rodney, DT, 1985-86-87-88
Lowery, Michael Z., FS, 1992-93; SS, 1994; LB, 1995
Lucas, Kenyatta C. (Ken), WR, 1997; CB-WR, 1998
Lucas, Thomas Edwin, RG, 1962; LT, 1964-65
Luke, Matthew B. (Matt), C, 1995-96-97-98 (co-c)
Luke, Tom, QB, 1989-90-91
Luke, Tommy, DHB, 1964-65-66
Lumpkin, John, g, 1916
Lyell, G. Garland, mgr., 1897
Lyerly, Frank G., mgr., 1921
Lyles, Sam, G, 1938-39
Lyons, Kenneth J., Jr., QB, 1971; 1973-74

Mc

McAllister, Dulymus J. (Deuce), RB, 1997-98
McAllister, Gerald, TB, 1987-88; CB, 1989
McAlpin, Harry Keith, OT, 1975; OG, 1976-77-78
McAnally, Jonathan D., trainer., 1996-97
McCain, Robert L., E-HB, 1944 (c); 1945 (c)
McCall, D. A., FB-QB, 1915-16
McCall, E. F., C-G-E, 1911-12-13 (c)
McCall, John W., RT-RH, 1908-09-10 (c)
McCardle, Chris, P, 1993
McCaulla, Michael E., trainer, 1976
McCay, David A., WB, 1994
McCay, Jim, FL, 1990
McClarty, W. H., G, 1918
McClure, Wayne L. (Mac), LB, 1965-66; DE, 1967
McClure, Worthy P., ST, 1968-69-70
McCool, Robert A. (Slick), FB, 1952-53-54

McCraney, James, E, 1966
McCrary, Conrad, Jr., DB 1979; LB, 1980
McDaniels, Bennie O., G-E-HB, 1918-19-20-21
McDonald, Quentin, DT, 1977-78-79-81
McDonald, W. Percy, FB, 1907; RE, 1909
McDonnell, Augustus H., LH, 1906
McDowell, James R., sub., 1898-99
McDowell, Ronald Brent, DB, 1998
McElroy, Brian, DB, 1984
McElroy, H. S., E, 1918
McFarland, Ben, sub-LE, 1898; 1900
McGarvey, John P., OL, 1998
McGee, Buford, TB, 1979-80-81-82-83 (co-c)
McGee, William C. (Carlisle), K, 1998
McGowan, David E., DT, 1993-94; DE, 1995
McGraw, Robert (Bob), DT, 1977
McIntosh, James T., RG, 1899
McKaskel, Jerry E., HB, 1955
McKay, Henry Earl, G, 1954-55-56
McKay, Rush, LT, 1960-61
McKellar, Frank Monroe, S, 1970; 1972
McKellar, George, mgr., 1958
McKellar, Milton Lane, mgr., 1965
McKey, Noel Keith, DE, 1971; LB, 1972
McKibbens, Thomas R., Jr., C, 1968
McKinney, Bob L., T-C, 1952-53-54
McKinney, David, QB,1984-85-86
McKinney, Ronnie, RB, 1988-89
McKinzie, Ralph Wm. (Mackey), DE, 1972; DT, 1974
McLean, George D., HB, 1894-95-96 (c)
McLeish, Thomas, TE, 1990-91-92
McLeod, Larry Mikell, OT, 1974
McLeod, W. N., LG-C, 1905-06-07
McMahan, Andy, trainer, 1997
McMillin, David, TE, 1982
McMurphy, Fred H., sub., 1899
McNeal, Theodis, DE, 1976-77-78
McPherren, Charles A., G, 1894-95
McQueen, Marvin Earl, Jr., E, 1964-65-66
McRight, Billy, HB, 1945
McWilliams, Howard, T-G, 1934-35

M

Mabry, Ed L., E, 1929
MacNeill, John B., C, 1973-74-75
Maddox, John Cullen, RE, 1963-64-65
Maddox, Milton Roland, trainer, 1959
Madre, John G., 1934-35-36
Magee, Anthony J., FS, 1997-98
Magee, Robert M. (Mike), WR-SG, 1965-66-67
Magee, Thomas Nakia, CB, 1994-95-96
Magee, William T. (Tommy), MM, 1969-70
Magruder, John M., QB-RH, 1901-02
Majure, Toby, HB, 1946
Malouf, Wm. A. (Bill), SE-QB, 1972-73; QB, 1974
Mangum, Ernest G. (Pete), FB, 1951-52-53
Mangum, Kristofer T. (Kris), TE, 1994-95-96 (co-c)
Mann, Ben F., T, 1946-47
Mann, William, HB, 1937-38
Manning, Elisha Archibald (Archie), III, QB, 1968-69-70 (co-c)

Manship, Doug J., FB, 1911
Markow, Gregory D., DE, 1972-73-74
Markow, Peter J., Jr., CB, 1972-73; SS, 1974
Marshall, Wm. D. (Bill), OG, 1973-74
Martin, Bobby, SE, 1986-87
Martin, Van, HB, 1924-25
Mask, James E., LE, 1950-51-52
Mason, James P., OT, 1972-73-74
Massengale, Kent, HB, 1937-38
Massengale, Marc B., C, 1978-79; OG, 1980
Massey, D. Brian, trainer, 1997-98
Massey, Charles Patrick, HB, 1949; mgr., 1951
Matthews, A. D., SS, 1986-87
Matthews, Elmer William (Bill), Jr., WB 1965-66-67
Matthews, James R., FB, 1952
Matthews, William L., sub., 1898
Mattina, Rodney A., LG, 1962-63-64
Maxwell, Harold L., LE, 1949-50-51
May, Arthur Wm. (Bill), DT, 1972-73
May, Christopher R. (Chris), OG, 1992-93-94-95
May, Doug, trainer, 1970
May, Jerry L., LG, 1951-52
Mayfield, Charles R., FB, 1917
Mays, Brian, NG, 1990-91-92-93
Meaders, E. L., LE, 1906
Meeks, James, trainer, 1979
Meeks, Jessie E., trainer, 1975
Meers, Mike, LB, 1993
Melton, James (Wesley), OT, 1990-91-93; OG-OT, 1992
Metcalf, Terrence O., OL, 1997
Metz, John Stephen, FB, 1964
Meyers, Dale, G, 1941-42
Mickles, Joe, FB, 1984-85-86-87-88
Mikul, Daniel P. (Danny), OG, 1971-72-73
Miles, Stephen D., DE, 1996
Miller, James G. (Jim), P, 1976-77-78-79
Miller, Jeffery A. (Jeff), OT, 1993; OT, 1994 (co-c)
Miller, Martin Van Buren, mgr., 1908
Miller, Michael T., SE, 1978
Miller, Romaro T., QB, 1997-98
Miller, Vernon Terry, Jr., LB, 1973
Millette, T. J., HB, 1950
Mills, Ralph, T, 1913
Mills, Wilmer R., C, 1964
Milner, E. C., Jr., mgr., 1959
Milstead, Don M. (Mike), C, 1968
Mims, Crawford J., RG, 1951-52-53
Mims, Gerald C. (Bubba), G, 1978
Mims, Marvin Taylor, C, 1964
Mitchell, Adam H. (Buddy), Jr., WT, 1968-69-70
Mitchell, Chris, DE, 1987; DB, 1988; SS, 1989-90 (co-c)
Mitchell, John I., Jr., G, 1959; 1961
Mitchell, Lansing L., Jr., mgr., 1972
Mitchell, R. P., mgr., 1909
Mitchell, Russell B., OT, 1980-81-82
Mitchell, Steve F., HB, 1909-10-11 (c)
Moffett, Timothy (Timmy), FLK, 1981; SE, 1982-83-84 (co-c)
Moley, Stanley Anthony, DHB, 1970-71-72
Moncus, Darrell A., C, 1992-93-94-95 (co-c)

Monsour, Thomas Joseph, LB, 1970; DE, 1971
Montgomery, Alvin D., mgr., 1982
Montgomery, Charles L., LT, 1950-51-52
Montgomery, John, HB, 1920-21-22-23 (c)
Montgomery, Lavelle, E, 1931-32-33
Montgomery, Tyrone, WR, 1990-91
Montz, Timothy S. (Tim), K, 1994-95-96
Moore, Artemus V. (Artie), RB, 1995-96
Moore, Hugh W., LT-C, 1907-08
Moore, Jeff, trainer, 1990-91
Moore, John, FL, 1989
Moore, Mark S., OT, 1979-80
Moore, Steven, DB, 1985; CB, 1986-87-88 (co-c)
Moreland, Brian, LB, 1977-78-79
Morgan, Gerald, QB, 1957
Morgan, Keith, mgr., 1982
Morganti, Charles, LT, 1951-52
Morphis, Rex, T, 1928-29
Morris, Ben, DE, 1984-85-86
Morris, Charles A., TB, 1960-61-62
Morris, C. H. (Bill), G-T-E, 1927-28-29
Morris, David C., QB, 1998
Morris, Gregory, WR, 1992-93
Morris, Herman, G, 1927
Morris, Jeremy D., DT, 1995-96
Morris, L. B., FB, 1918-19
Morris, Sheldon A., WR, 1997; HB, 1998
Morrow, George C. (Buz), DT, 1967-68-69
Mosby, Herman Wm., SG, 1969-70
Moses, Ronald David, DE, 1970-71
Moses, Samuel S. (Rollo), Jr., RG, 1963-64
Moss, Charles E., Jr., FS, 1974; RCB, 1975-76
Moss, Edgar, C, 1903-04
Moss, Howard, DB, 1984; SS, 1985-86-87
Motton, Kyron A., LB, 1994-95
Mounger, E. H., 1895
Muckle, Wayne, OG, 1989
Muirhead, Allen, RH, 1951-52-53-54 (co-c)
Muirhead, Jack, LB, 1989; OLB, 1990-91; DE, 1992
Mullins, Roy Lee (Chucky), FS, 1989
Mullins, Tim, trainer, 1988-89-90
Murff, Dan E., TB, 1973; CB, 1974-75
Murphey, Greg, mgr., 1990-91-92
Murphree, Tom, E, 1937
Murphy, C. E., G, 1914
Murphy, Harvey A. (Ham), E, 1938-39
Murray, Hugh, mgr., 1962
Muse, Carl W., FLK, 1975
Mustin, John W., HB, 1923-24-25 (c)
Mustin, Robert Wm. (Billy), HB, 1946-47-48-49
Myers, Charles William, QB, 1964-65
Myers, L. D., G-T, 1911-12; 1914
Myers, Mark, trainer, 1986
Myers, Ricky, SE, 1985-86
Myers, Riley D., SE, 1968-69; 1971 (co-c)
Myers, William D., FB, 1899 (c); 1900 (c)

N

Nabors, Jeremy, mgr. (video), 1997-98
Nasif, George Milid, Jr., CB, 1974-75-76
Neely, Charles Wyck, WB-TB, 1968; DHB, 1969-70

Neely, Paul, FB, 1915-16
Nelson, Charles (Tex), C, 1933-34-35
Nelson, James Mitchell, LG-LB, 1963-64-65
Nelson, Josh A., QB, 1994 (co-c); 1995
Nesmith, Malcolm Dwayne, LB, 1981-82-83 (co-c)
Newcomb, Mac, WR, 1984
Newell, Ronald Bruce, S, 1965; QB, 1966-67
Nichols, Rodney J., trainer, 1974
Nicholson, Quintila D. (Moine), RB, 1994-95
Niebuhr, Robert Bryan, OT, 1974; DLT, 1976; MG, 1977-78
Noblin, Jeff, DB, 1984; FS, 1985-86
Norman, Charles R. (Chuck), P, 1965-66
North, Roy, E, 1934
Northam, Larry Ray, DT, 1970; OT, 1971; TE, 1972
Nunn, Freddie Joe, DE, 1981-82-83-84 (co-c)

O

Odom, Edcardo B. H. (Ed), WR, 1995
Odom, Jack L., E, 1947-48
Olander, Carl John (Bubba), OG, 1976-77
O'Malley, Sean, NG, 1991-92-93
O'Mara, B. B., C, 1918; 1921
Orr, Deano, OLB, 1990; LB, 1991; DE, 1992; FB, 1993
Osgood, Chris, QB, 1985-86
Oswalt, Robert J. (Bobby), QB, 1946-47-48
Otis, James C., DE, 1979-80-81; LB, 1982
Ott, Dennis H., G-T, 1952-53
Ott, Reggie, FB-HB, 1951-52
Ott, Timothy A., DT, 1978
Owen, Bryan, K, 1985-86-87-88 (co-c)
Owen, Joe Sam, FB, 1969
Owen, Joe Sam, II, CB, 1996-97
Owen, Robert L., WG, 1968
Owen, Sam Walton, LG, 1961-62
Owens, Darrick, SE, 1990; WR, 1991
Owens, Robert L., T, 1957-58-59

P

Pace, W. Reginald (Reggie), C, 1974-75-76 (co-c)
Panzarella, Anthony E., NG, 1993; DT, 1994
Parham, David Howard, OG, 1971-72; OT, 1973
Parish, Randy, mgr., 1989-90-91
Parker, Edd Tate, E-T, 1951-52-53
Parker, Thomas, E-T, 1936-37-38
Parkes, James C., Jr., C, 1966-67-68
Parkes, Robert S., RCB, 1976
Parkes, Roger B., CB, 1973
Parks, Hugh Harold (Hank), SE, 1970
Parrott, Reggie, LB, 1987-88-89-90
Partin, Alan Wayne, OT, 1981-82
Paslay, Lea C., HB -QB, 1951-52-53; 1956
Patch, Dan, QB, 1944
Pate, Jeff, mgr., 1986
Pate, Joey, mgr., 1983-84
Patridge, C. K. (Dewey), FB-RH, 1957-58-59
Patridge, Stewart D., QB, 1996-97 (co-c)
Patterson, Hunter, mgr., 1997
Patterson, Jerome, T, 1915

Patton, Elack Chastine, HB, 1894
Patton, Houston, QB-HB, 1953-54-55
Patton, James R. (Jimmy), Jr., HB, 1952-53-54 (co-c)
Patty, J. W., E, 1927-28-29
Payne, I. J., E, 1928-29-30
Peabody, Greg, K, 1987
Pearce, Rex, HB, 1944
Pearson, Markee T., FS, 1998
Pearson, Thomas H. (Babe), LT, 1947-48-49-50
Peel, John, DE, 1977-78-79
Peeples, Everett U., E, 1928-29-30 (c)
Pegram, James Allen, TE, 1975
Pennington, Gerard M. (Jerry), RG, 1976
Perkins, A. P., G, 1923-24
Perkins, Charles G. (Charlie), OL, 1997-98
Perkins, James B., Jr., RG-mgr., 1905-06
Perkins, P. A., sub., 1904
Perry, Leon, Jr., FB, 1976; TB, 1977-78; FB, 1979
Perry, Mario, TE, 1984-85-86
Perry, Monty, OG, 1989-90
Peters, Michael J. (Mike), TB, 1993-94
Peters, Ned, HB, 1934-35-36
Peterson, Cory S., WR, 1996-97-98
Pettey, Thomas J. (Joe), E, 1962-63-64
Pettis, William S., Jr., mgr., 1900
Pfeffer, W. L., FB, 1907
Phenix, Patrick J., OT, 1979-80-81-82
Phillips, Forrest C., Jr., mgr., 1979-80-81
Phillips, Hermon B., E, 1947
Philpot, Cory, RB, 1991-92(co-c)
Pierce, Richard Wayne, C, 1982-83-84
Pierce, Tommy, mgr., 1983
Pigford, W. L., mgr., 1917
Pilkinton, Sam T., T-G-E, 1905-06; 1911
Pittman, James Bradley (Brad), CB, 1974; SS, 1975-76
Pittman, Thomas Michael (Mike), DT, 1974-75-76
Pitts, Quintin, TB, 1984
Pivarnik, John, T, 1940
Plasketes, George M., QB-DE 1975; DLE, 1976 (co-c); DE, 1977 (co-c)
Poole, Calvin Phillip, G, 1946-47-48
Poole, George Barney, LE, 1942; 1947-48
Poole, Jack Lewyl, E, 1948-49
Poole, James E. (Buster), LE, 1934-35-36
Poole, James E. (Jim), Jr., TE, 1969-70-71
Poole, Oliver L., T, 1946
Poole, Ray S., RE, 1941-42; 1946 (c)
Poole, Ray S., Jr., TE, 1976
Pope, Carl Allen, TB, 1965
Popp, Romeo, FB-QB, 1939-40
Porter, James Edward, FB, 1970-71-72
Porter, Frank, FB, 1983; DB, 1984; SS, 1985
Portis, Michael, DE, 1982; NG, 1983-84-85 (co-c)
Posey, H. H., 1895
Potts, Ed, G, 1930
Powe, Alexander, M., QB, 1908
Powell, Eric, FS, 1986
Powell, Kelly Newton, QB, 1981-82-83 (co-c)
Powell, Kenneth W., RG, 1960
Powell, Travis, mgr., 1962
Powers, Jimmy T., T, 1954

Prater, Charles, OLB, 1988
Preston, Roell, WR, 1993-94
Price, Charles, E, 1930
Price, Don, CB, 1986-87-88-89
Price, James Richard, LG, 1958-59-60
Price, Jarratt, FB, 1978-79
Priestly, Harry D., Jr., 1897 (c)
Prince, T. J., G, 1925-26
Pritchett, Kelvin, NG, 1988-89; DT, 1990 (co-c)
Provencher, Shannon K., OG, 1994-95-96
Pruett, Billy Riddell, C-G, 1955-56-57
Pruett, Dawson, C, 1987-88-89-90 (co-c)
Puryear, H. H., G, 1911-12

R

Radford, Jimmy W., mgr., 1973
Ranatza, Michael A., C, 1974
Randall, George M. (Buck), FB, 1961-62-63
Randolph, Vivian, QB, 1911
Ratcliff, Culley C., HB, 1920
Rather, Edward, mgr., 1939
Ray, E. H. (Red), C-HB-T, 1917; 1918 (c); 1919
Ray, Joe, FB, 1982
Ray, S. T., FB, 1974
Rayborn, Jerry Joe, E, 1963
Rayburn, Tony, OG, 1984; OG-C, 1985 (co-c)
Redhead, John A., Jr., sub.-RT, 1898-99-1900
Reed, Benton, DT, 1983-84-85
Reed, Edwin, WR, 1979
Reed, Garland R. (Randy), TB, 1969; TB-FB, 1970; TB, 1971
Reed, James M., TB, 1973-74-75
Reed, John B. (Jack), QB-S, 1951-52
Reed, John E., mgr., 1907
Reed, Robert E., HB-QB, 1997
Reed, S. Leroy, Jr., LH, 1955-56-57
Reeder, Herbert, E, 1931
Regan, George Bernie, E, 1959
Reid, Ed, RT, 1924; QB, 1925
Reiley, Marion W., RT, 1903
Renshaw, Paul, sub., RE-QB, 1906; 1908-09
Reyes, Tutankhamen M. (Tutan), OT, 1996-97-98
Reynolds, Robert R., 1916
Rhodes, Jeff, OG, 1986; OT, 1987-88; OG, 1989
Rice, Alfred L. (Al), LB, 1996-97-98
Rice, Tommy, mgr., 1963
Richards, Tyrone, FB, 1976-77-78
Richardson, Jerry Dean, LE, 1965-66-67
Richardson, John A., FB, 1964-65
Richardson, Marion L., (Mel), Jr., LB-DE, 1972-73
Richardson, Ricky, DE, 1986-87; OLB, 1988-89
Richardson, William, T, 1933-34-35
Richmond, W. M., 1895
Richter, Todd, FS, 1985
Ricks, W. B., mgr., 1898
Riddell, T. H., C-HB, 1919-20
Roane, Ralph H., LT, 1900
Robbins, Michael D. (Mike), TB, 1966-67
Roberson, J. Lake, Jr., RG, 1938-39-40
Roberson, Shed H., E, 1932-33-34
Roberson, Shed H., Jr., RG, 1958-59

Thomas, Frederick L. (Fred), CB, 1994
Thomas, James Larry, LB, 1968; MG, 1969
Thomas, Jim Earl, RB, 1987; TB, 1988; RB, 1989-90
Thomas, Kelvin D., SS, 1998
Thomas, LeMay P., WR, 1992-93-94-95
Thomas, Marquise, OLB, 1991; DE, 1992
Thomas, Roville (Bobo), DB, 1980
Thompson, Keith, DE, 1987; OLB, 1988-89
Thompson, Robert, G, 1925
Thompson, Robert P., RH, 1898
Thompson, Robert W., G, 1919
Thompson, Steve, trainer, 1990
Thornton, Chester, TB, 1979
Thornton, James Ray, E, 1951
Thornton, Johnny H., DT, 1978
Thornton, Nathan, RB, 1991-92-93
Thorsey, Frank, E, 1940-41-42
Tiblier, Jerome J., FB-RH, 1944; 1947-48
Tillery, Douglas W., FB, 1962
Tillman, James Shannon, FB, 1938-39-40
Tillman, Ronald, TB, 1965
Timmons, Aaron, HB, 1944
Tipton, Julius R., RE, 1893-94
Toler, Kenneth P. (Ken), SE, 1978-79-80 (co-c)
Tomaso, Mike, trainer, 1998
Torgerson, Larry Donald, OG, 1968; DT, 1969-70
Totten, G. C., 1924
Townes, Clarence Henry, HB, 1894
Townes, Jack A., mgr., 1964
Townsend, Andre, DT, 1981-82-83 (co-c)
Trainer, Orlando K., NG, 1994; OG, 1995; OT-DT, 1996
Transou, Lewis, mgr., 1940
Trapp, Franklin Wm., LB, 1966-67-68
Trapp, Lee H., G, 1930-31-32 (c)
Trauth, Marvin H., LT, 1950-51-52
Travis, Brent, mgr., 1989-90
Traxler, David, OG, 1977-78-79
Trimble, William, G, 1933
Trotter, Trafton A., FB, 1993-94
Trotter, William C., LH-LE, 1907-08; 1909 (c); 1910
Truett, George W., E, 1952
Truitt, Eric, DB, 1982-83-84; CB, 1985
Tuggle, Jimmy, FB, 1952
Turnbow, Guy, T-FB, 1930-31-32
Turner, Christopher (Chris), TE, 1991-92-93-94
Turner, Gary W., DE, 1973-74-75-76
Turner, John H., Jr., LG, 1964
Turner, Thomas N., G, 1929
Tyler, Breck, FLK, 1980-81

U

Upchurch, Robert K., C, 1961-62-63
Urbanek, James E. (Jim), RT, 1965-67
Ussery, Flint L., LB, 1994
Uzzle, Robert H. (Bobo), DE, 1966-68

V

Vacca, Richard W., DE, 1979
Valverde, Charles, LG-LE, 1907-08

VanDevender, Wm. J. (Billy), MM, 1968-69-70
Vandevere, Wm. E., E, 1911-12
Vann, Clay, OLB, 1990; DE, 1992
Vann, Thad (Pie), T, 1926-27-28 (c)
Vargo, Curt B., mgr., 1995
Vaughan, Robert C., DT-WT, 1965-66-67
Vaughn, Gerald, CB, 1989; SS, 1991; FS, 1992
Veasley, Jeremy, FB, 1992-93
Veazey, Burney S. (Butch), TE, 1971-72-73
Vega, Chad, mgr., 1990-91-92
Vincent, Keydrick T., OL, 1997-98
Vinson, David L., C, 1993-94-95 (co-c)

W

Wade, Robert Myers (Bobby), FB, 1965-66-67
Wade, Todd M., OG, 1996; OT, 1997-98
Wainwright, Ralph, C, 1899
Wakefield, Victor Reed, Jr., LCB, 1973; TB, 1974
Walker, Donald, trainer, 1977-78
Walker, Gerald H., HB, 1928
Walker, Gregory Scott, TE, 1981-82; TE-OT, 1983; OT, 1984
Walker, Harrison Carroll, Jr., QB, 1965-66
Walker, Harvey W., QB, 1926-27-28
Walker, Paul L., mgr., 1973
Walker, Richard H., G, 1922-23
Walker, Terrence C., OG, 1975; OT, 1976-77-79
Wallace, Daniel D. (Dan), mgr., 1995-96-97-98
Wallace, James M., LHB, 1900
Wallis, James H. (Jimmy), QB, 1967-68; MM, 1969
Walls, Wesley, DE, 1985-86-87; TE-DE, 1988 (co-c)
Walsh, Willie Henry, MM, 1970; SS, 1971; RCB, 1972
Walters, James A., T, 1953-54
Walton, Byron S., RE, 1910-11
Wamble, James E., LB, 1976
Wander, Mose, mgr., 1933
Ward, Harry, mgr., 1926
Ward, Jesse Davis, LE, 1937-38
Ware, Cassius, LB, 1992-93
Warfield, Gerald Wayne, MM, 1964-65; S, 1966
Warner, Jack, QB, 1945
Warren, Homer E., HB, 1916
Washington, Quincy J., DE, 1997
Watkins, Dennis R., RT, 1976; OG, 1978
Watkins, Thomas B., QB, 1900-01; 1903
Watson, Bill E., G-T, 1949-50-51
Watson, Henry D., Jr., RE, 1907
Watson, R. Virgil, G-T, 1914; 1916
Watson, Thomas C., QB, 1904
Wayne, Nathaniel (Nate), Jr., LB, 1994-95-96-97 (co-c)
Weatherly, James D. (Jimmy), QB, 1962-63-64
Weathers, Curtis L., TE, 1974; 1976-77-78 (c)
Webb, David B., trainer, 1998
Webb, Hunter (Buddy), G, 1942
Webb, Jay, DE, 1984-85 (co-c)
Webb, Luther Wade, FB, 1970; DT, 1971
Webb, Reed S., WG, 1966-67
Webster, Edgar, sub., LE, 1903-04-05
Weese, Norris Lee, QB, 1971-72-73 (co-c)
Weiss, Richard T., 1952-53-54-55

Weiss, Richard, Jr., OG, 1978
Welch, Thomas P. (Toby), mgr. (video), 1997-98
Wells, David Kent, WB, 1963-64-65
Wells, Matthew E. (Matt), LB, 1995-96-97
Wells, Vernon, QB, 1945
West, Carl E., FB, 1950-51
West, John Wayne, LT, 1955-56-57
Westerman, Richard W., HB, 1950-51-52
Westmoreland, Daniel, TE, 1989-90
Wettlin, D. G., QB, 1906
Whitaker, David, T, 1942
Whitaker, Murray P., OT, 1976-77-78
White, Abner, C, 1990-91
White, Brad, FB-HB, 1931-32-33
White, Brad, CB, 1978-79-80
White, Hugh L., C-LG, 1898-99-1900
White, James Thomas, FB, 1960
White, John U., Jr., OG, 1974
White, Lloyd, G, 1936-37
White, Robert P. (Randy), OG-C, 1975; C, 1976; OG, 1977
Whitener, Larry J., G, 1966-67
Whiteside, Lance, CB, 1991-92
Whiteside, Paul L., HB, 1951
Whitten, L. D., E, 1917
Whittington, John, HB, 1938
Whittington, O. M., 1921
Wicker, Brian K. (Kyle), LB, 1993-94-95; DE, 1996 (co-c)
Wicker, Reginald K. (Trey), TE, 1993; DE, 1994-95 (co-c)
Wigley, Daniel, DT, 1986-87-88-89
Wilburn, Barry Todd, DB, 1981-82-83-84
Wilcox, Reuben D., HB, 1927-28-29
Wilford, Dan S., E, 1961
Wilford, Ned B., E, 1961
Wilkins, Ernest, RG, 1905
Wilkins, Joseph T., III, LE, 1962-63-64
Williams, Amzie J., LB, 1997-98
Williams, B. Frank, QB, 1907
Williams, Bill T., 1937
Williams, D. E., 1895
Williams, David Wayne, G, 1981
Williams, Don N., RE, 1955-56-57
Williams, Freddie Lee, TB, 1976-77-78; WR, 1979
Williams, G. H., G, 1920
Williams, Gary Neil, LB, 1971; DE, 1972
Williams, Horace, LE, 1953
Williams, J. M., 1921
Williams, John, trainer, 1983-84
Williams, John C., Jr., G, 1954-55
Williams, Ken, OL, 1988; OG, 1989
Williams, Malcolm, RB, 1998
Williams, Murray L., Jr., ST, 1968
Williams, Nakita, LB, 1979-80-81-82
Williams, Robert J. (Ben), DT, 1972-73-74; DT-MG, 1975 (tri-c)
Williams, Robert W., DB, 1980
Williams, Sebastian (Snake), OLB, 1989; DT, 1990-91; OT-DT, 1992
Williams, Tyler C., DT, 1998
Williamson, John D. (Hotshot), T, 1926

Williamson, Terry, NG, 1982-83-84
Wilson, Charles (Buddy), C-E, 1933-34
Wilson, David G., 1934-35-36
Wilson, Frank M., TE, 1993-94-95
Wilson, G. Davis, OL, 1997
Wilson, Quentin L., DT, 1995; DE, 1996
Wilson, Robert, HB, 1946-47-48-49
Wilson, Stacy E., DL, 1991; DE, 1992-93-94
Windham, Donald W., RG, 1962-63-64
Windham, John, E, 1925-26
Winfield, Paul E., SS, 1994; LB, 1995
Winstead, Bobby Ray, SG, 1968
Winstead, Jimmy LeRoy (Jim), TB, 1971; FB, 1972; TE 1974
Winston, Lowell, T, 1957
Winter, Michael Todd, trainer, 1988-89-90-91
Winther, Richard L. (Wimpy), C, 1969-70
Wise, Billy, TE, 1978-79-80
Wisozki, Ray, T, 1941
Wohlgemuth, John T., TE, 1970; OT, 1971
Wonsley, Nathan, TB, 1983-84-85 (co-c)
Wood, Andrew, RE, 1906-07 (c)
Wood, Charles G., C, 1971-73
Wood, Dan, C, 1941-42 (c)
Wood, Meredith, HB, 1930
Woodruff, James Lee (Cowboy), HB, 1957-58-59
Woodruff, Lee T. (Cowboy), FB, 1927-28-29
Woods, Joe, WR, 1992-93
Woods, Kenneth (Kenny), SS, 1998
Woodward, H. G., QB, 1923
Woodward, Ray, HB, 1942
Worley, Michael S., SS, 1992-93-94
Worsham, Jerry Dean, G, 1963
Woullard, Reginald, SE, 1975; TB, 1976-78-79
Wrenn, R. B., C, 1914-15
Wright, Trenton (Trent), SS, 1996-97
Wyllie, Phillip, LB, 1978-79-80

Y

Yandell, Robert (Bobby), HB, 1941-42
Yarbo, Welborn, T, 1916
Yelverton, Billy G., E-T, 1952; 1954-55-56
Yerger, J. S., FB, 1903
Yerger, Wm. G., sub. 1903
Young, Carl R., G, 1949-50
Young, John Wm., Jr. (Bill), SE, 1970-71
Young, Mark, QB, 1985-86-87-88

Z

Zanone, Curtis, J., mgr., 1974
Zeppelin, Deron, TE, 1987; OL, 1988
Zullo, Michael, mgr., 1985-86